Sai...

CURIOSITIES

DAVID GOSS

NIMBUS
PUBLISHING

To two of my young Walk 'n Talks friends that I hope will carry
my stories to the next generation—
Jeremy Keats and Jessalyn Wright.

Nimbus Publishing Limited, PO Box 9166, Halifax, Nova Scotia, B3K 5M8, (902) 455-4286, www.nimbus.ca

Printed and bound in Canada
Nimbus Publishing is committed to protecting our natural environment. As part of our efforts, this book is printed on 100% recycled content stock.

Design: Margaret Issenman
Cover photo: Rob Roy Productions, Saint John, NB
Cover design: Heather Bryan

Library and Archives Canada Cataloguing in Publication

Goss, David
Saint John curiosities : stories and histories from David Goss.
ISBN 978-1-55109-687-2

1. Saint John (N.B.)—History. 2. Saint John (N.B.)—Anecdotes. I. Title.
FC2497.4.G67 2008   971.5'32   C2008-904607-2

We acknowledge the financial support of the Government of Canada through the Book Publishing Industry Development Program (BPIDP) and the Canada Council, and of the Province of Nova Scotia through the Department of Tourism, Culture and Heritage for our publishing activities.

Contents

Along the River 88

West of the River   130

Foreword

Saint John has a rich, colourful, and very long history. Whether your starting point is in its fossilized geological formations, its early discoveries and explorations, or the beginning of the municipality with the arrival of the American Loyalists, there are thousands of stories that could, and should, be told.

This book continues the fine tradition of earlier and current local authors with dozens of new stories. Saint John and its surrounding area have yielded such a treasure trove of stories that this hodgepodge of unusual, strange, and delightful information will fascinate you for hours.

This miscellanea of Saint John tidbits takes you from Carleton to Lancaster, and from Greenhead to Martinon. It is a happy marriage of information from the deep recesses of our past and the recent years of the twenty-first century.

You will learn all about the local Algerines, a term from the early nineteenth century that is considered derogatory, but is still used in Saint John today. The story of Cassie Hassie might make you wonder who today's kids might pick to replace her. From the stories of who or what can be found in old and new burial grounds, to the shooting of buffalo in the Wild West city of Saint John, some bits of information may sound familiar, but have never been told in such detail. Lobster canning started here, as did the medicinal use of anesthesia for surgery. You probably did not know that there are more than sixteen sites on the West Side that have been visited by ghostly apparitions. Did you know that gypsies had their own settlement in the area?

What about Boggs Corner—can you identify where it is? You will discover the location of Paddy's Flats, Rayne's Beach, and Avery's Corner. The text reveals that the first Saint Johner to play in the NHL did not do so until 1972, and that the famed Boston Red Sox was the first major league baseball team to visit the Maritimes, right here in Saint John.

Saint Johners have never considered themselves isolated from their neighbours, and this book follows in the same vein. It includes stories about Rothesay, the Hammond River, and the upriver communities of Nerepis and Grand Bay too.

The readers of *Saint John Curiosities* are well served by this delightful treasure of David Goss's tidbits!

Harold Wright
May 5, 2008

Acknowledgements

The author thanks all those who, over the past fifty years, have shared the anecdotes contained in *Saint John Curiosities*.

Unfortunately, many of you are nameless, as I have lost track of who told me what, where, and when while conducting so many public events over the years; however, you will recognize your stories, and I want you to know I am grateful you shared them—and the readers will be too.

Specifically, I'd like to thank Harold Wright, who was so kind in helping me check facts on many items that do not have printed sources. The staff of the Regional Library in Saint John, the Archives of the New Brunswick Museum, and the microform section at UNB Fredericton were extremely helpful.

Bill Thompson and John Geffken, fellow researchers at the Saint John Library, led me to several of the curiosity finds—in fact, more than I could ever follow up on.

Finally, thanks to Dan Soucoup of Nimbus for suggesting this work, and to editors Patrick Murphy and Caley Baker for their guidance through the writing and editing process.

And to you, dear reader, for your continued interest in our history through your purchase of the books that I have been able to author.

David Goss
May 7, 2008

Image sources

Joe Stone, 2

City of Saint John Recreation Deparment, 7, 33, 183

Duffy Collection, 21

Jackie Clark, 26

Crosby Molasses, 42

Saint John Energy, 47

National Film Archives, 60

Audrey Straight & Marg Long, 63

Norman Wasson, 66

Saint John Tourism, 70

Edith Stewart, 87

Rowan Collection, 97

Connie Cunningham, 111

Rod Daley, 116

Garry Maxwell, 156

Terry Keleher, 171

Ann Baker, 174

Peter Garner, 178

All other images courtesy of David Goss

East of the River

Saint John's history stretches back to the explorations of Champlain in 1604. Champlain rejected the area for his settlement and resided for only ten months on Dochet's Island in the St. Croix River (where New Brunswick and Maine meet today). In 1645, the La Tours had a fort in the harbour, but no further activity is recorded as having occurred until Simonds, Hazen, and White came to the area as pre-Loyalist settlers in 1763. Their impact on the area as loggers and quarrymen might have been minimal if not for the American Revolution and the influx of settlers that resulted in 1783, which saw an instant city created where the St. John River meets the Bay of Fundy. Some of these settlers were assigned lots on both sides of the harbour, while others travelled inland to the banks of the St. John and Kennebecasis rivers. It is these areas that are the focus of *Saint John Curiosities*.

This section explores the east side of the harbour—what is today central Saint John, the North End, and what was long known as Simonds, or Saint John East. Central Saint John grew largely on the strength of merchants who owned ships, bought goods from around the world, and sold them throughout the province. The area burned in 1877, but the wealth that had been accumulated by these merchants was sufficient to allow the city to rebuild quickly. The structures they built are known today as the best intact collection of Victorian buildings

Trinity church's 210 foot spire, shown here circa 1956, is the tallest point in what is now known as central city, and the Trinity Royal Preservation District.

in Canada, and are very much a part of the city's attraction as a tourist destination.

The North End grew as it was the location of the riverboat service for the merchants of the city centre. Saint John East owes its existence and growth primarily to shipbuilding, based first at Marsh Creek, and later on Bayside Drive. The days of shipbuilding are gone—today the area is *the* place to shop in Saint John, though the city centre is still well supplied with shops and merchants, too.

A whale of a tale

Look up Abraham Gesner on the Internet and you will find that he is the man who discovered kerosene, and is sometimes described as the father of the oil industry. Sources may also say that he founded what is now the New Brunswick Museum, and that he completed the first geological land surveys for the province in the 1850s. It is unlikely, though, that you will find the story of how Gesner was fooled by a Saint John trickster named Robert Ray.

The year was 1839, and whaling was still part of the seafaring life in Saint John. Ray placed the jawbone of a whale in a stack of cordwood waiting to be cut at Market Square. When the unknowing sawyer began to cut the bone, he complained of the hardness of the "wood," but persevered. It took him an hour to cut what he would usually do in minutes, and his saw was dulled greatly. When the sawyer discovered that he had been cutting bone, not wood, he drew the matter to the attention of Dr. Gesner, who wondered which shipment of wood it had come in with. After being told it had come from Grand Lake on a scow, the doctor examined the bone and declared it the shin bone of a mastodon. He then visited Grand Lake several times to try to find other bones, but of course without success. Dr. Gesner wrote newspaper articles about the find, and it became the subject of much scientific curiosity; however, the truth about the bone soon leaked out, much to the chagrin of the good doctor.

Holidays and soirees at the Admiral Beatty Hotel

When the Admiral Beatty Hotel opened for business in June 1925, it quickly became the centre of social life in Saint John; it remained so until the Delta and Hilton hotels opened in 1981 and 1984, respectively.

For the Christmas season in 1926, the Admiral Beatty's old-fashioned dinners and dances were advertised and given coverage in the local press. Promotions for the hotel's New Year's Eve celebration (signed by the manager, H. Arthur Peters) promised a fifteen-piece orchestra, souvenirs for the ladies and gents, and

Postcard of the Admiral Beatty Hotel

a midnight surprise, and assured that "nothing would be omitted to make the celebration the best ever." The *Saint John Globe* described the hotel's Georgian ballroom as "gaily decorated with evergreen streamers wound with silver tinsel draped about the walls and suspended from the chandeliers." Such celebrations continued until the hotel closed on November 22, 1982.

Happy to be nabbed

On the night of March 31, 1847, horrible noises emanated from the palatial Bank of New Brunswick on Prince William Street. Some said the noises sounded like a howling dog, while others thought they might have come from ghosts that haunted the building. Still others believed it was a human crying, "let me out, let me out."

Upon being roused, the caretaker would not come to the bank, thinking that the noises were part of an April Fool's joke. Eventually, concerned citizens got the attention of the bank's president, Thomas Leavitt, who opened the building. Inside, not a soul could be found, but the sound could be heard plainly on the second floor. Soot seen falling into the huge fireplace indicated that someone was trapped inside the chimney.

A would-be robber, almost dead from his efforts to crawl up onto the roof, was happy to have been discovered. His rescuers lowered a rope to him from the roof, but the crook was too weak to grasp it. Masons had to be called in to chip him out of the chimney.

According to some accounts of the attempted robbery, the thief was a sailor who thought he could navigate the chimney, then let his friends in the windows so they could rob the bank and leave Saint John richer for their daring. Writer Dan Soucoup found an account that identified the thief as John Slater, a man claiming to be a baker who thought he was slim enough to squeeze down the chimney. Some versions of the incident say the man escaped on the spot, while others say he escaped when he was brought to trial a few weeks later.

No matter which version is true, if the burglar had gotten to the valuables in the vaults, the Bank of New Brunswick may have folded long before it did in 1913. The bank is no longer in business, but its successor, the Bank of Nova Scotia, rebuilt on the site, and the new building looks as formidable as the old.

Loyalist landing shocker

On August 22, 1988, American writer William Randall shocked Saint John heritage buffs when he came to the city to talk about his personal search for his Loyalist roots. Randall, who had spent eight years researching the Loyalist story and published four books on the matter, told the audience there were many myths that needed to be dispelled—for example, the idea that Canada was the first choice for the Loyalists, when in fact they preferred parts of Maine and Ohio.

That night, Randall's most astounding statement was that Market Slip was not the first landing place of the Loyalists in New Brunswick. He said they most likely came ashore at Smuggler's Cove at Sheldon's Point, which was then a remote place, but is now an easily accessible part of the Irving Nature Park. As proof he used letters that told of how the 1783 settlers cut through thick forest for a week, then came to a position where they could see the Bay of Fundy, the Reversing Falls, and the fortifications of Fort Howe. The place that offered this view to the Loyalists could be the present-day Wolastoq Park (the Centracare site), or the seventy-two-metre hill later chosen for Martello Tower. Randall's revelation did not change the popular perception that Market Slip is the place where the Loyalists landed. Whether or not Market Slip was the very first landing place for the Loyalists, they did eventually arrive there.

Barbour's General Store

Built in 1860, Barbour's General Store began life as Bridges' Store at McGowan's Corner in Sheffield. In 1967, the building was loaded onto a barge, floated down the St. John River, through the Reversing Falls, and out to Courtenay Bay. It was moved by truck to the corner of King Street East and Carmarthen Street.

Peter Stokes, Canada's foremost restoration architect, selected the King Street East location for Barbour's because of its proximity to the Old Burial Ground, the ancient County Jail, and the venerable County Courthouse. Barbour's manufactured spices, extracts, peanut butter, King Cole Tea, Morse's Tea,

The United States Marine Corps Band, July 4, 1984, in Market Square where the Barbour's General Store stood for twenty-five years

and was to celebrate its one hundredth birthday (along with Canada) in 1967. Due to urban renewal the company moved its manufacturing operations to Sussex in 1966, but wanted to maintain a presence in Saint John; thus the Barbour's Store was a centennial project.

Barbour's president, Ralph Brenan, decided on the project—the store with its range of goods from yesteryear—when he discovered that his granddaughter did not know what coal was, and realized there were a lot of other mercantile items from his childhood that she would not recognize, either. To ensure that it was a genuine throwback to the past, Brenan consulted with historian Huia Ryder who "dug into every attic and cellar in the Maritime provinces" when stocking the store with items representative of a general store of 1867.

The store was moved to its next location at Market Square, west of Water Street, in 1981 to complement the redevelopment of the area. In 2008, the store was moved to the corner of Water and King streets, the area that Saint Johners know as the foot of King.

A cacophony in the cupola

In 1791, William Thompson donated the first bell to sound the hours from the cupola of Trinity Church. In an era when few had watches of their own, most folks found the sound of the bell helpful—it ensured they arrived at work on time in the morning and told them when to go home at night. But there were times when its ringing was not welcome. One such occasion was reported in the *Morning News* on January 6, 1841:

The tongue of this bell, (at this present writing 3 o'clock, Monday) appears to have got loose; for it is, and has been, for the last two hours, alarming the whole city by its confounded noise. We cannot, for the life of us, ascertain the meaning of such a tingling! We pity the poor man that pulls the string. He has a hard time of it unless he has a deputy. Sometimes it appears as if both he and his deputy were pulling together. They pull very well together judging by the noise they make. Either they or the bell must be cracked; we fear the tongues and sides of it will have to be greased for next Sunday; for they must corrode by friction. We wish it were the fashion to muffle the bells, then we would not be bothered with such a confounded din.

Complaints about the bell continued into the next century. Archdeacon Arthur Caulfield often spoke of guests of the Admiral Beatty Hotel, adjacent to old Trinity, calling the church to complain that the Westminster chimes that rang on the quarter hour disturbed them, and that the bell ringing on the hour, especially at ten and eleven o'clock and midnight, kept them from sleeping.

Sammy the Salmon
swims atop Trinity Church

Every summer in downtown Saint John, tourists are seen looking up ninety metres (almost three hundred feet) at the golden salmon atop the weathervane on the spire of Trinity Church. From Germain Street, it is difficult to guess how big the gilded fish really is. To demonstrate that the salmon is really about two metres (six feet) long, staff at the church made a papier mâché fish and introduced it to the public in the summer of 2006. Visitors soon named him Sammy.

The model fish was used many times during public presentations that explained that the weathervane is both a symbol of Christianity (the early Apostles were fishermen and the fish was a secret symbol), and a tribute to Saint John's salmon and the men who fished for them. At one presentation in July 2006, a photocopied image of two men who had taken the fish down for maintenance in 1928 was passed through the crowd. To the great surprise of the guides, one man among the listeners that night said, "Hey, that's my father in that photo." The man was Fred Willar, and at a public presentation in the summer of 2007, Fred donated the original photo to the church to help the guides tell its story.

Beliveau's "cannonball blast"

The Saint John Forum on lower Main Street overlooking Marble Cove was built in the winter of 1932, and was destroyed by fire on March 20, 1967. One of the best-known events to take place at the Forum during its thirty-five years of existence was the Canadian hockey championship competition between the hometown Saint John Beavers and the Quebec Aces for the Alexander Trophy in 1952.

Jean Beliveau of the Aces was without a doubt the most

C.E. (Nick) Nicolle, a teammate of Beliveau's, was a high scorer for the Beavers hockey club in the 50s, and in the 70s and 80s oversaw the growth and expansion of a recreation service that was able to support the Canada Games of 1985

watched player in that series. He was described in the *Evening Times Globe* prior to the five-game series as "one of the greatest and in some quarters reputed to be highest paid hockey player in the world." When the series opened in Saint John, another writer noted that Beliveau was known for his shot, a "cannonball blast that tears holes in wire screens, and cracks rink boards."

Many claim that Beliveau's shot did break the boards in Saint John, but according to Beavers' player Nick Nicolle, who did some serious scoring during the series, none of Beliveau's shots were that destructive. Just in case his memories of that series fifty-five years ago were faulty, Nicolle decided to check his hockey scrapbooks for a reference to a particularly damaging Beliveau shot, but found none. He feels that the press, who covered the series thoroughly in Saint John and Quebec, surely would have noted such an incident. The series ended in Quebec, as the Beavers lost four games to one.

The count and the court case

The ornate deBury mansion, built in a commanding position high on a ridge overlooking Main Street at Harrison Street is one of the city's most interesting architectural delights. The fact that it was once owned by a count only adds to its allure. Count Robert Ferdinand Dieidimus Visart deBury was a Belgian nobleman who traced his ancestry to the Crusades. He was said to be of the highest rank, and a descendent of an English family who emigrated from the lower countries at the beginning of the sixteenth century. He maintained homes in England, Belgium, and Saint John. His move to Saint John in 1883 was the result of his marriage to Lucy Gertrude Simonds, a native of the city, in Germany four years earlier. The couple had twelve children.

After coming to Saint John he took British citizenship, and served as counsel for Belgium and France. He and his wife owned land and other homes in the area surrounding their mansion in Saint John. These holdings included houses in Millidgeville, and on Douglas Avenue, Portland Street, Main Street, Harrison Street, and Simonds Street.

Count deBury's wife predeceased him by a year. When he died on August 31, 1907, at the age of fifty-nine, his estate was said to be valued at ten thousand dollars—about a quarter million dollars today! He bequeathed the house and property on Main Street to his son, Robert, but left everything else in the care of his lawyers. The money remaining after their expenses would be used to support Count deBury's daughters. A court case followed as there were claims against the estate that had not been settled and it dragged on until 1911. These claims included requests for expenses by lawyers that had worked for the count collecting rents at his various properties; wages owed to domestic servants he employed; irregularities found in his books, which were not balanced correctly; ground rents he had not paid on property his wife held prior to her death; and rents on properties that were owed by occupants, which had not been collected for one reason or another (hardship or bankruptcy)

The deBury House of Main Street still stands

during the count's lifetime, but which his successors wished settled to their advantage.

The court case undoubtedly changed local opinions of the count—though he had a title, he was flesh and bone like the rest of us, and chose to live among the common folk of Saint John.

A decorated war heroine

Near the main doorway of the Dennis Knibb Auditorium in Saint John High School is a plaque that identifies a heroine of World War One—nurse Agnes Louise Warner. Warner was the recipient of the Médaille d'Honneur in bronze, the Médaille Militaire, and the Croix de Guerre. On April 5, 1919, the *Saint John Globe* wrote "perhaps no woman in the war has received more recognition from the French government than the St. John lady."

Letters that Warner wrote home describing her adventures in France from August 2, 1914, to January 1, 1917, were published in a book titled *My Beloved Poilus*. In the now-rare book she writes of having one hundred men under her care, and of being as "sleepy as a dried apple." Warner says she has mixed feelings when she hears that the troops have left Saint John, but later notes the Twenty-sixth Battalion of New Brunswick has "a great reputation here and St John can be proud of them."

Warner's letters are also studded with notes that clearly show the folks back home were supportive of her efforts on the front: "A check came today from the De Monts chapter I. O. D. E. [Imperial Order of the Daughters of the Empire]...it touches me to tears," and in another she writes, "the box from the

[Victoria] high school girls came today, and it was like having Christmas all over again."

My Beloved Poilus, which included a preface by clergyman and famed author Hiram A. Cody, sold for one dollar and went through five printings in 1917. Today, the book still provides a glimpse into what Saint Johners experienced during a long ago war in a faraway place.

Cellar-dwelling Red Sox hit the field in Saint John

On August 26, 1930, the Boston Red Sox, great favourites of Saint Johners, played in the city and narrowly defeated a team of locals by a score of 7-5 at the Shamrock Grounds. The game marked the first time a major league team had ever played in the Maritime provinces. The local nine had ten hits against the big league pitching. Right fielder Art Graham was the leading Saint John hitter with a double and a single in four at-bats. The game, which took one hour and forty-two minutes to play, had all the hallmarks of great baseball—twenty-one scattered hits, sacrifice flies to advance runners, stolen bases, and double plays. In addition, both pitchers were strong and each team committed only one defensive error.

At the time of the game in Saint John, the Boston team was deep in the cellar of the American League with forty-three wins and eighty-one losses with a month left in the major league season. Nonetheless, they were a professional team, and the old North End Diamond was packed with Saint Johners who cheered vociferously for the local nine. The Sox remained in the cellar that year, finishing the season with only fifty-two wins, which, of course, did not include the exhibition game played in Saint John.

Harbour rumours

The activities of ships from around the world in the harbour have long been the lifeblood of Saint John. The city has fought hard to overcome the idea that high tides, the reversing effect at the falls, heavy fog, and underwater ledges make Saint John Harbour difficult to sail into. For the most part, city officials were able to set the record straight among sea captains and pilots, so it was with some chagrin they read an incorrect report in a Boston newspaper on December 24, 1849, claiming the harbour had frozen over, though this had never happened before or since. The misinformation was contained in a letter written by James F. W. Johnson, which read: "I left St. John this morning on my way to Boston. The frozen harbour of St. John and the cold and stormy season of the year had laid up all the steamers along the coast. I had no other recourse, therefore, but to face the severity of the weather and proceed by land."

Officials moved quickly to refute the gentleman's statement, but of course, there were some individuals who could not be convinced that ice never forms in the harbour.

Open to interpretation

Almost everyone recognizes the bronze sculpture in King's Square of world champion speed skater Charlie Gorman as a fine piece of art. Moncton-based artist Claude Roussel's sculpture portrays a very realistic human figure in a skater's pose, and hints at the speed Charlie was known for. Children often reach up and touch Charlie's skate blades to see if they are as sharp as they look.

The Roussel sculpture that adorns the outside of the council chamber at city hall, just down the hill at the foot of King Street, is another matter altogether. Roussel won a competition to design the three-piece sculpture for the outside of the building when it opened in 1971. Roussel's sculpture has been called various names over the years, and is often referred to as the "eyebrows" of city hall. Some say that the three-piece sculpture, which hangs over the edge of the roofline, is designed to direct hot air out of the council chamber—and sometimes there is a lot of hot air in that locale.

Bernard Cormier, city cultural affairs officer, says Roussel intended the sculpture, which is officially named *Progression*, to resemble a

Roussel's monument to Gorman, the famous speed skater, still stands in King's Square

"flower on the lapel of a dull grey suit," and to "add a little colour to the drab and unexciting façade of the city hall building."

Cormier is able to laugh at other interpretations of Roussel's work. "Some people," he explains, "say it reminds them of the three levels of government, with their fingers dipping into our pockets!"

The other *Cutty Sark*

Saint John once had its own version of the *Cutty Sark*, the famous British ship built in 1869. It is quite amazing that the Saint John version was built at all, for the age of sail had long since passed by the time it was constructed in 1919. The *Cutty Sark* was one of the last three vessels built at Marsh Creek in the Courtenay Bay yard of Grant and Horne. It was a four-masted schooner, weighing about 686 tons and measuring 55 metres (181 feet) long, though different sources give varying figures. The *Cutty Sark* was constructed by a fourth-generation shipbuilder named R. C. Benson from Bear River, Nova Scotia, who was brought to Saint John by the ship's owners, the New Brunswick Shipbuilding Company. The vessel was floated and sent on its maiden voyage to the Canary Islands with a cargo of lumber in 1919. At its launch the owners referred to their *Cutty Sark*'s more famous predecessor, so it was not through ignorance that the second ship ended up with the same name. Unlike Saint John's *Cutty Sark*, which burned off the coast of Nova Scotia on June 12, 1929, the original vessel can still be visited at Greenwich, England, today.

Love at the spring

A monument under a perpetually dripping rock face adjacent to 11 First Street identifies the site as Jenny's Spring, the place where famed English writer William Cobbett met his wife-to-be, Anne Reid, in 1785. Cobbett, who was stationed at nearby Fort Howe, wandered by the well on a frigid winter morning, and spotted Anne scrubbing out a washtub in the icy water. He told the companion he was walking with that the girl would someday be his bride, although Anne was only thirteen years old, and he was twenty-one at the time.

When Cobbett was transferred from Fort Howe back to duty in interior New Brunswick, he gave Anne 150 guineas so she could use the money to move away if she ever became uncomfortable in her father's house, for he was a heavy drinker and known to beat his wife. The Reid family subsequently returned to England, after which Anne left home, and took on the job of servant to Captain Brasiac. When Cobbett returned to England and came to claim his bride, she returned the 150 guineas he'd given her. They were married in 1792.

The couple then moved to America, where William Cobbett began his writing career. Writing that he considered satirical was seen by others as cutting and acrimonious, and he was given the nickname of *Peter Porcupine*. After returning to England around 1800, Cobbett was jailed for his comments. Anne stood by him through it all, and bore seven children of which five (one girl and four boys) lived to adulthood. It would seem that Cobbett knew a good woman when he saw one on that cold winter morning at the First Street spring. He described the first six months of their marriage as "the happiest six months of [his] life." It's a great love story, but it does not explain how the spring came to be named Jenny's Spring, and not Anne's Spring!

Coffee by candlelight

Long before Tim Hortons spread to Saint John, a coffee house that stood at the foot of King Street was the place for the men of the community to carry out business, catch up on the latest news, and of course, enjoy a coffee. Cody's Coffee House, located on the west corner of King and Prince William streets, opened in 1803.

Owner William Cody advertised memberships at a cost of twenty shillings per year. For that sum, members had access to a "London paper published three times a week, and New York and Boston daily paper, and a Saint John weekly paper," at the shop, and Cody provided "full candlelight." He also promised a pen, ink, and the use of a blank book for his members to record local news. Cody ran the coffee house for twenty years before moving to Loch Lomond and opening Ben Lomond House. In 1853, the King Street structure was torn down, and the Imperial Building was erected on this important business corner. The Imperial Building burnt in the fire of 1877, and the Bank of Montreal was built on the site. The ornate structure stands today as the cornerstone building of the Irving CenterBeam Place.

A crime against
the county courthouse

At almost two hundred years old, the Saint John County Courthouse on Sydney Street at King Street East overlooking King's Square has a storied history, but few know that its demise almost occurred before it was one hundred years old.

In 1919, the courthouse burnt so badly that the council of the day called for razing what was left, despite the fact that the building's unique unsupported three-storey spiral staircase survived the fire with no damage. Insurance carried at the time was ten thousand dollars, and it was going to cost seventy-nine thousand dollars to rebuild the courthouse. To make room for the proposed larger, modern building, which would house all civic officials and include a public auditorium, the 1840 Fire

The County Courthouse, pictured far right, c. 1915

House south of the courthouse would have been torn down. Local lawyers and visitors from across Canada and the United States who thought that razing the Georgian structure was short-sighted protested city council's plan. Council listened, and decided to rebuild, rather than raze, the structure.

A potent pick-me-up

James I. Fellows was one of a dozen Saint John men who created cure-all medications in the nineteenth century. He began his apothecary work with his father, Israel, at the corner of King and Germain streets in Saint John. One night the Fellows used one of their most potent medicines, Dyspepsia Bitters and Speedy Relief, to aid firemen fighting a blaze in Flaglor's Alley. The medicine quickly revived the firefighters' fatigued bodies—and drove them into the street seeking water to quench the burning in their bellies.

Sketch of James I. Fellows

Testimonials about the effectiveness of Fellows' potent creation were widely printed, and orders for the product came from across the continent. The sales of his medicine made James Fellows a wealthy man, and he eventually left the apothecary business. He went to London to serve as agent general for New Brunswick, promoting products the province was manufacturing. A relative of Fellows, Jack Alston, wrote the family's version of how the Dyspepsia Bitters came to be: "Fellows was apprenticed to a chemist in New York and he invented the concoction from his employer's stock, and used it as a pick-me-up for himself and friends after bouts of heavy drinking." He added that the story has been passed on verbally, its truth unverified.

Alston also shared the ingredients of Fellows' Compound Syrup. Each teaspoon contained:

> 1 mg strychnine hydrochloride
> 3 mg quinine sulphate
> 20 mg calcium hypophosphite
> 8 mg iron pyrophosphate
> 8 mg manganese hypophosphite
> 8 mg potassium hypophosphite
> 8 mg sodium hypophosphite

The syrup's label carried the following instructions:

> Dosage—Adults, 1 tsp in a wine glass of water, three times daily, before meals as tonic. Caution—contains strychnine and quinine. Take only as directed or as prescribed by a physician. Indiscriminate use may cause untoward disturbances.

A work of art history

In 1983 the Saint John Bicentennial Commission asked local artist Fred Ross to create a mural as a legacy gift to the city on its two hundredth anniversary. Ross's mural, *The DeLancey Encampment*, was placed on permanent display in what was then called the Aitken Bicentennial Exhibition Centre. To create his representation of the city's history from the Loyalist perspective, Ross used local citizens—Bernard and Elizabeth (Volney) Cormier, Robert Duplisea, Peter Gillies, Greer (Stackhouse) Gillies, Richard and John Claus, and Basil Vautour—as models. The mural features the first mayor of Saint John, Gabriel G. Ludlow, who was a colonel of one of the DeLancey's Brigade Battalions during the American Revolution, and contains many religious references, including the Madonna and Child, the Adoration, the Last Supper, and the Servant and the Wine. Fred Ross also included the figure of a Dalmatian in *The DeLancey Encampment*. At the time of the mural's unveiling, Moosehead Breweries was running a promotional campaign called "Spot the Dog," and many mistakenly thought Ross's Dalmatian was one of the dogs the brewery expected its customers to find.

The sound of Saint John takes the world by storm

On September 14, 1893, the *Saint John Globe* reported that twenty-three members of the City Cornet Band were boarding a train that evening and heading to Chicago for the World's Fair.

Several thousand people showed up at the train station to see them off, and the City Fife and Drum Band played as they boarded the train. In Chicago, they were met by several Saint Johners living in the city and escorted to the La Salle Hotel.

At the fairgrounds, twelve thousand people showed up to hear the City Cornet Band play, and it was reported by the press that they "attracted more attention than any other band performing on the grounds." At the hotel, the band staged a reception for three-dozen Saint Johners. They treated them by playing Saint John composer E. G. Nelson's "My Own Canadian Home."

In 1948, the City Cornet Band celebrated its seventy-fifth anniversary. Bandsman J. Vincent Mudge recalls that at that time the band was "nearing the end." Mudge says the band gradually ceased practicing sometime in the early 1950s. He still has a broken slide trombone and several of the bandsmen's uniforms in his theatrical equipment studio on Winter Street, where they serve as reminders of one of Saint John's great bands.

The right way

The order for New Brunswickers to switch to driving on the right side of the road as of midnight on November 30, 1922, presented a great challenge for Saint John businesses. Those who were still delivering coal, milk, bread, ice, and other products door-to-door by wagon found that their horses had trouble adapting to the new rules. They would often return from a delivery to find that their horses had returned to the left side of the road. Eventually the animals did pick up on the change, though not before a few incidents that proved scary to both man and beast.

The change also posed a challenge for the New Brunswick Power Company, as the doors on its streetcars now opened into the middle of the road, rather than next to the curb. The company had thirty cars to remodel, which meant that it had to begin work long before the deadline. As a result, for a short period of time the cars had doors that opened on both sides of the chassis, which exposed passengers to danger. Temporary work was done so the doors on the right side would not open prior to the official switch to the right side of the road.

On November 30 at midnight, a "large force of men" came to the car barns on Wentworth Street to make the final changes to the streetcars, so they could safely take to the streets the next morning. Streetcars continued to run in Saint John until

Horses continued to be used in 1968 as this photo of Spring Clean Up shows

1948, when many of them were sold. Some were sold to other cities, while others were bought by individuals who wished to use them as cottages. Still other cars were left to rot in various locations around Saint John. One of the cars can still be seen at the Canadian Railway Museum in Saint-Constant, Quebec. A few years ago it was featured on an eighty-eight cent stamp produced by Canada Post. Saint John streetcars live on!

A mighty cold Communion

Three thousand members of Saint John's Roman Catholic population celebrated the first Mass at the Cathedral of the Immaculate Conception, which was still under construction on Waterloo Street, on December 25, 1855. There was no heat or light in the building, which was said to be still only two-thirds complete when it was finally consecrated in 1885. The fervour and dedication of the crowd that Christmas Day in 1855 is difficult to imagine today, when the slightest hint of bad weather is enough to cause people to skip church. On January 5, 1856, the *New Brunswick Courier* reported that during his sermon, Bishop Connolly referred to "the great efforts which had been made during the past three years by the Catholics of St. John," to ensure that the cathedral was completed. Locals had donated twenty-two thousand pounds for the cathedral's construction. Connolly called the cathedral "an ornament to our city, and a fitting monument to the unparalleled benevolence and religious enthusiasm of our Catholic fellow citizens."

Uplifting words after a terrible collapse

George and Mary Narraway Bond were a well-known couple that made a lasting impact on Saint John; though it has been over 150 years since they died, we can cite their contributions to society without much trouble. George is known for a poem that he wrote to commemorate the tragic collapse of a 1,400-foot bridge that spanned the St. John river from Watson Street, Carleton, to Merritt Street, Portland, on August 8, 1837. Seven men lost their lives when the bridge fell into the harbour. The poem reads, in part:

> What solemn scenes attract our wond'ring eyes!
> What melancholy news salute our ears.
> The lofty fabric, towering to the skies
> Rear'd for the use of man in future years.
> Fell in a moment in the wat'ry deep
> The sound thereof spread terror all around
> In wild confusion some were seen to weep
> And crowds of mourners in the streets were found.

Bond may have gained inspiration for the poem as he accompanied his wife, Mary, while she consoled the grieving families in Saint John West, where she was a preacher. Most of Mary's work, which was rare for a woman at the time, was done from a Sabbath school at Sand Point. She worked among the poorest of the poor children, and also with sailors who came into the port. George ably assisted Mary, who continued to preach for thirty years. Although no record of Mary Bond's sermons exists, surely some Saint Johners could trace their spiritual roots back to the good work she did during the first half of the nineteenth century.

Growing up in the Grotto

The dictionary describes a grotto as a picturesque cave, or an artificial cave popular in gardens, but when the term was used to describe the rundown housing that existed below Fort Howe from Main Street to the harbour in Saint John, it was not meant to be complimentary. Russell Cowan, an expert commentator on the area who grew up in the North End, described his boyhood home of the 1930s, and its derogatory nickname, in an article that appeared in the *New Brunswick*

The tightly packed North End where the grotto was located

Historical Society Bulletin in 1986. He described the Grotto as "thickly settled with a large number of typical three-storey, box-like houses…built closely together to provide shelter." Cowan wrote that those who lived in the houses had either left behind "crowded conditions" in Europe, or "worn out hilly farms" in southern New Brunswick, and were seeking better lives for themselves and their children.

He ended his report on a positive note, writing that the children who had grown up in dismal conditions in the Grotto had come to be "leaders in the community, its business and professional life," and had made "name[s] for themselves in other parts of the continent." These now-grown children spoke proudly of the sacrifices their parents had made while living in the Grotto. Cowan also wrote that the area's derogatory name had disappeared, and so had its homes, swept away by urban renewal in the 1960s.

From Slaughterhouse Hill to Smiling Pool

When Ruby Cusack moved to East Saint John in the 1960s and began teaching in local schools, she asked her students to find out as much as they could about the area, thus she became acquainted with some of the old place names that were beginning to disappear then, and are all but gone today. Here are a few:

- The Flats—Name given to the Courtenay Bay mud flats before the causeway to uptown Saint John was built in the early 1960s.

- Mary Ann's Place on Rock's Hill—Found on a shortcut to the north of the Flats that joined Bayside Drive (called Red Head Road by many) to Thorne Avenue.
- Crouchville Treasure—Name given to pirate treasure found on the shore of Courtenay Bay.
- Parish Hall—Located at 139 Bayside Drive, the hall served official functions when county councils existed prior to 1967.
- Dutchman's Lake—Received its name because a Dutchman was said to have drowned there. It was located behind the Parish Hall, and was filled in to become the East Saint John Diamond, a great spot for softball.
- Edith Avenue—Named for Edith Magee, who gave music lessons at her home on the street.
- Labourer's Union Bell—Originally called folks to work in downtown Saint John. It was placed in Stella Maris Church when it was built in 1924 to call parishioners to Mass.
- Pottery Hill—Now called Mount Pleasant Avenue, the street received its original name because several potters lived and worked there.
- McAvity Corner—Refers to the McAvity family, who dealt in furs, feathers, foxes, and hens. The corner was on Bayside Drive where the Jervis Bay Legion is now located.
- Lee Brickyard—The brickyard, located on Bayside Drive at Little River, won international fame for the bricks that were created there using clay from the banks of the river. In 1875, a council in London, England, insisted that their new market be constructed of Lee bricks from Saint John.
- Likely's Beach—One of many good seashore locations to swim, found parallel to Bayside Drive between Little River and Red Head Corner. Likely's took much gravel and sand off the beach for construction purposes until it was pro-

hibited to do so by provincial environmental legislation of the late 1970s.

- Slaughterhouse Hill—Runs down from McDonald Street toward Courtenay Bay. Cattle were marched from the uptown Saint John ship terminals to the McDonald Slaughterhouse.
- Pott's Cove—Ships were built at Pott's Cove, located on Courtenay Bay, opposite East Saint John School.
- Sandy Bottom, Mud Bottom, Gravel Shore, Deep Hole, and Smiling Pool—Five swimming holes on Little River that many East Saint John boys frequented. According to Gar Bovaird, the favourite was Smiling Pool because of the way the sun danced off the water—and it was secluded enough for skinny-dipping!

Halloween hijinks

Many people recall the custom of Halloween parades in Saint John, when throngs of colourful costumed characters moved along Charlotte Street and down King Street past the Woolworth Store.

A column penned by indefatigable and popular writer Ian Sclanders for the *Saint John Evening Times Globe* on November 1, 1933, described one of the popular parades as "stupendous… the greatest production of the year." According to Sclanders, who was destined to become a senior editor at *Maclean's Magazine* from 1955 to 1966, shouts of "whooooo, booooooo," were raised by young and old, as they "did their rounds…begging candy, apples, cakes and nuts."

The parades became a bit boisterous, and in 1968 Woolworth's plate glass windows were smashed in. It seems the parades weren't officially quashed at that time, but they did die out following the incident. Unfortunately, both Sclanders and Halloween hijinks are long gone from the Saint John scene.

The keeper of the well

One of the last places in Saint John where residents could get cold, clear water from a well was the campground area of Rockwood Park. In the 1960s, the water source was nicknamed Hanley's Well. William Hanley told interviewer Valerie Evans that his name was originally attached to the well as a joke, but over time it became official. From 1953 to 1981, he was the chief guard at the lock-up (located at 124 King Street

Summer view of Lily Lake, near Hanley's Well, c.1960

East). Hanley explained: "Sometimes it was pretty sad to lock up some of the poor fellows, so every Friday night I would get two bottles of rye and take the ice-cold well water from here and try to forget about the job. If there was a problem at the jail (and there usually was on Friday night) the police knew exactly where to find me." Eventually they began to call the spot Bill Hanley's Well.

Though Hanley was retired at the time of the interview, he said he still went to the well to drink the water, and usually took a bottle home with him. Bill Hanley concluded the interview by sharing an anecdote about a tourist who came to the well to fill her jugs. According to Hanley, she walked over to him and a friend and asked if they knew the Hanley that the well was named after. Hanley continued: "The other fellow said it was me. She wanted to know how much she owed me for the water. We all had a great laugh, and then she took our picture."

What the Dickens!?

In November 1867 while en route to North America, Charles Dickens was contacted by the merchants of Saint John, who asked if he would include a visit to the city in his schedule. At the time, Saint John was a rival to Montreal and Toronto, and the fourth-largest ship-owning port in the world, so it would have been natural for Dickens to consider visiting during his North American tour. Dickens had not been to the city during his previous trip to this side of the Atlantic in 1843, though he'd been in the Maritimes and stopped in Halifax.

Dickens knew a bit about Saint John; however, he did not know how to spell the city's name properly, as seen in chapter 21 of *Little Dorrit*. In this serial novel, Dickens wrote of one Mr. Sparkler, the only child of a Mrs. Merdle. Mrs. Merdle had lived in Saint John when she was married to a colonel who served at Fort Howe, and her son was born in the city. Dickens's description of her son was not complimentary—he called the boy "chuckle headed," and wrote that he had been given "few signs of reason." The reason for his condition was that "his brain had been frozen up in a mighty frost which prevailed at St. John's, New Brunswick, at the period of his birth there, and had never thawed from that hour."

Dickens never did come to the city. He had worn himself out as he travelled across America, with three-hour recitations of *A Christmas Carol* night after night, and with the ten- to twenty-mile walks he loved to take each morning. He had also continued bickering with American publishers who were pirating his work without paying him a cent. He did come to Canada, but only to Ontario and Quebec. Though he made a tour of England in 1868, it was obvious his health had been much strained by his North American tour. He died just two years later in June 1870.

The importance of one tiny *s*

The Prince of Wales, another well-known Englishman named Charles, called the city by the wrong name 116 years after Dickens made the same mistake. This occurred during the bicentennial visit of Charles and Lady Diana, Princess of Wales, on June 16, 1983. With a huge crowd present at Loyalist Plaza at Market Square to greet the royal couple, speeches were, of course, expected. Prince Charles said: "On behalf of my wife and myself I thank St. John's for your kind and indeed warm welcome."

An audible groan was heard from the crowd, but the prince continued his remarks with no further mispronunciation of the city's name. Later, he made private apologies to citizens he met, and to the organizers for his error. Everyone took it in stride, having gotten quite used to this mistake over the decades.

Bibles and beer

The alleyway between the Bank of Nova Scotia and St. Luke's Anglican Church, which joins Main Street to Metcalfe Street in the North End, was once known as Brewery Lane. The bank stands on the site of what was once J. & J. Keltie's Brewery, according to Roe and Colby's 1875 map of the Portland area, which amalgamated with Saint John in 1889. The map identifies homeowners and businesses, and is an invaluable aid to understanding how the area looked long ago. It also shows how Saint John was laid out before the Great Fire of 1877. According to the map the home of Reverend Canon William G. Harrison, rector of St. Luke's church, stood on the north side of the brewery. It must have seemed strange to those passing up and down busy Main Street to see Reverend Harrison passing down Brewery Lane on his way to the hall of St. Luke's Church to prepare for services.

Colonel Tucker's legacy

Over the years, the location of the University of New Brunswick, Saint John (UNBSJ) campus in the Millidgeville area of the city has been described as Tucker Park. The story of Tucker Park begins in the late nineteenth century, when Colonel J. J. Tucker made his fortune as an agent in Saint John for Lloyd's of London. He lived downtown at 1 Chipman Hill, a property that survived the Great Fire of 1877 and still stands today. The ornate door created by famed woodcarver John Rodgerson for the Tucker home still stands at the entry to the house. Tucker's Chipman Hill residence was a convenient place for him to do business, but his real love was his country estate, located high atop a hill overlooking the Kennebecasis River, where UNBSJ is situated today.

Upon his death in 1914 Tucker willed his country estate to the City of Saint John. His wish was that an English garden would be established on the site, but he left no bequest for such a thing; however, his sister, Caroline, gave the city ten thousand dollars for the garden two years later. The city sat on the money until the depression years, when they used the funds to create a make-work project that would develop a road through the park connecting Sandy Point Road to Kennebecasis Drive. Parts of that road can still be walked to this day, but when the money ran out, no more work was done to develop the property as Tucker and his sister had wished. The City donated eighty-seven acres of the four-hundred-acre Tucker Park to the university for its Saint John campus on May 13, 1966. Though a couple of chestnut trees that are said to have stood outside Tucker's cottage remain on the property, the garden he dreamed of was never developed.

The Macy's of the Maritimes

There were more than a few tears shed on December 31, 1973, as the doors of Manchester Robertson Allison (MRA), the Macy's-like department store on King Street in uptown Saint John, closed for good. Six months later in the June issue of the *Atlantic Advocate*, Dorothy Dearborn wrote: "The death of MRAs was more than the death of a department store. It marked the end of a way of life in the city, a loss of a meeting place for hordes of shoppers and it broke a link with the past which had seemed destined to last forever."

During its 107-year history, there was only a 10-year period (between 1948 and 1958), during which the store was not owned by Saint John businessmen. The Saint Johners who owned the business kept up with the latest trends in New York

The King Street facade of MRA's

and England, and MRA's gained loyal customers both at home and across the country.

Among the store's innovations was the introduction of a live Santa Claus to the children of Saint John on Saturday, December 17, 1887. So many people showed up to catch a glimpse of Santa from outside the store's plate glass windows that management had to pull the blinds down, and the police were called to disperse the crowd. According to *Santa Claus: A Biography*, by Winnipeg author Gerry Bowler, there is not known to have been an earlier department store Santa in Canada. While MRA's was not the first Canadian department store to stage a Santa Claus parade (the Eaton's parade in Toronto in 1905 was the earliest), they held the first in the Maritimes on November 19, 1951. Though MRA's no longer exists, the parade is still held each year and might be said to be the store's legacy in the city.

When the store closed Lloyd MacDonald, its last manager and a forty-year employee, told Dorothy Dearborn, "We had a lot of good, faithful customers." It seems they would to this day, if the store still stood.

A home to lay their heads

Kent Marine Hospital, the first hospital in the province, opened in 1822. The wood-frame building on Britain Street was rented from Nehemiah Merritt. Its operation was financed by a one penny per ton levy on any vessel weighing more than sixty tons that entered any port in the province. During the Great Fire of 1877, to the chagrin of many, the tired and worn hospital was one of only a few buildings saved by Mr. Barnes's bucket brigade. The hospital's inadequacies were soon recognized, and the Dominion government built a new structure in 1882.

Mariners only used the new Kent Marine Hospital for eighteen years, until it proved more cost-effective to transfer them to the General Public Hospital. The building was vacated in 1900, and land baron William Wallace Turnbull then provided the funds to establish the Saint John Home for Incurables. In 1937 the building was renamed the Turnbull Home to honour the donor whose gift was the largest that had ever been made by an individual in the city.

The Turnbull Home still provides enhanced services for those who live there during their last years, and five generations of the Turnbull family have continued the work that William Wallace Turnbull began over a century ago.

Caught on tape

When forty-one-year-old Torontonian Fred Esson's 42-metre (152-foot) climb up the inside ladder of the chimney at the McAvity plant on Rothesay Avenue went awry, he became the subject of the first same-day broadcast of a dramatic rescue by a local television station.

Esson was four and a half metres (fifteen feet) from the top of the chimney when three of the rungs on the interior ladder broke under his weight. He continued to scramble to the top, where he leaned over the twenty-three-centimetre (nine-inch) ledge and gasped for air. Once his situation became known, crowds began to gather, and a six-hour-long drama unfolded. He was finally rescued when an RCAF helicopter from Greenwood, Nova Scotia, arrived on the scene. Its twenty-four-year-old pilot, J. C. Smith of Winnipeg, manoeuvred the helicopter into place while his twenty-two-year-old assistant, former Saint Johner R. L. Baxter, lowered a rescue basket to Esson. Esson clambered in and hung on as the pilot skilfully raised him from danger, then landed the helicopter in the rear yard at the McAvity plant.

A crowd of thousands was on hand to watch the rescue, and probably just as many saw it at home on television that night. The incident was filmed by Art Cody of CHSJ-TV, which had first gone on the air on March 24, just a few months earlier. The event demonstrated the drama that could be captured using this new medium.

Sweet, sticky success

The Crosby Molasses Company's plant stretches along Rothesay Avenue, and is one of the few food manufacturers left from the old days in Saint John, a city that once had dozens of such factories. Crosby's is the only molasses manufacturer still operating in Canada.

The company began in Yarmouth, Nova Scotia, in 1879. L. G. Crosby, who was then trading lumber and fish in the West Indies, was looking for cargo to bring back to the Maritimes on his empty ships. He found the product he was looking for in treacle, the dark, rich syrup extracted from mature sugar cane that we know as molasses.

Initially, the treacle arrived at Yarmouth in oak casks; the

Crosby's trucks have long been a presence in Saint John

business was moved to Saint John after 1896 to expedite shipping to inland markets. Today, it comes by ship and is pumped into 2.75-million-gallon storage drums overlooking the Digby Ferry Terminal at Beatteay's Beach on Saint John's West Side. As it is needed, the molasses is brought by tanker truck to the Rothesay Avenue plant, which opened in 1911. It is processed and packaged by the fifty-plus employees who work there, and the sweet-smelling and sweet-tasting product is sent all across Canada directly from Saint John.

The history of a heritage home

The cottage that Henry Bowyer Smith had constructed for his bride, Charlotte LeBaron Hazen, at 68 Carleton Street is one of Saint John's grandest and oldest homes, and one of the city's earliest brick buildings. They were the first couple married in Stone Church, just across the street from their cottage.

The home remained in the family for fifty years. In 1894 it was bought by James F. Robertson, one of the three owners of the venerable Manchester Robertson Allison Department Store. Robertson used the home as his winter residence, and escaped to his Shadow Lawn property in Rothesay for the summer. Robertson added the conservatory, which makes the building so distinct from others in the downtown.

In 1939, the Benevolent Protective Order of Elks bought the property and completely redecorated it. In 1945 a serious fire destroyed the second floor of the house, and total damage was stated at thirty thousand dollars. The building was next owned by Fundy Broadcasting, and became the home of CFBC, the leading radio station in the city at the time. The broadcaster, flush with revenue, added the CFBC stained glass windows that remain to this day. The ghost of station owner Senator Neil McLean was said to have visited the house during this era. He was also one of the owners of Connor's Brothers sardine packers, and his ghostly countenance was always recognizable because of a fishy odour that arose when he visited the station. CFBC left the building in 1995 and the United Church of Canada has owned it for the last decade.

The laws of hockey—
Saint John-style

Over the years hockey evolved from the game known as hurley that was played primarily on outdoor rinks. By 1895, Saint John teams were hosting teams from Quebec City, Montreal, Charlottetown, and Halifax, and were also travelling to those areas to play; however, to build skills most of the games were still played locally. In 1895, the president of the local City Amateur League was C. Walter Clarke. The "Laws of Hockey of the City Amateur League" stated that the league's goals were to "improve posture, to perpetuate the game of hockey in Saint John, to protect it from professionalism, and to promote the cultivation of kindly feelings among the members of the hockey clubs." All players had to be "*bona fide* residents of St. John."

The laws provided extensive instructions for how to proceed when the puck went off the ice and into the snowbanks of the outdoor rinks the games were played upon. The goalkeeper could not "lie, kneel or sit upon the ice" during the game, and instead had to remain in a standing position. Games were to be "two half hours with an interlude of 10 minutes between," and once a game began, the seven initial players chosen to play were the only seven that could be involved in the game, except for "reason of accidents or injury...or for other reasons satisfactory to the referee," whose decisions, the laws noted, "shall be final."

Saying goodbye to a city symbol

For many years the Loyalist man was used throughout Saint John as a symbol of the city's heritage. Towering, three-metre-high (ten-foot-high) versions of the figure stood over the billboards at the gateway to the city to welcome visitors.

When George Teed died on the last weekend of December 2007, a vocal opponent of the demise of the Loyalist man symbol was removed from the scene. For years George had fought the gradual removal of the long-time symbol of the city's founders. Though the claim that Saint John is a Loyalist city was and is an honest one, there is no denying that one must honour all of the groups, including the Native, French, Scottish, Irish, and Jewish communities, who were involved in building the city as it is today.

Teed recalled that the idea of the Loyalist man origin-ated during a meeting at the Manchester Robertson Allison Department Store in the late 1950s to decide on a symbol that would set the city apart. Seward McDonald came up with the concept of the Loyalist man, and artist Jim Stackhouse fleshed out the idea. Eastern Sign's Ron

Ron Howard's version of the Loyalist man

Howard probably painted the Loyalist man on more billboards than anyone else over the years. Ray Butler, a tourism officer with the City of Saint John, increased the use and popularity of the figure with his drawings for pins and promotional kits, letterhead, and envelopes.

It is rare to see the figure on today's literature, and there are only two or three Loyalist men still visible around the city. It seems that these figures will not be replaced when their colours fade.

Boom and bust

As portions of Saint John began to undergo urban renewal in the 1960s, a survey of employers in the area was conducted. Of the fifteen businesses that were identified as major establishments on the survey, only two are still in downtown Saint John today. The following businesses have now disappeared from the area:

- The Barbour Company, which made tea, spices, and other goods, and employed 190 people, was located at 17 North Market Wharf, in the buildings where Grannan's Seafood Restaurant is located.
- Acadia Wharf, where the *Princess of Helene* (the ferry to Digby) docked, employed 125 people. The Hilton Hotel stands on the wharf today.
- E. S. Stephenson & Company's machine shop on Dock Street employed 75 workers. The New Brunswick Electric Power Commission had a generating plant on Dock Street at Union Street, which employed 25 people.

Main Street Saint John, December 1969. All the buildings on the left are now gone

- Seventy people worked at National Drug's facility on Mill Street.
- Also on Mill Street, 175 workers packaged Red Rose Tea for Brooke Bond and Company.
- At Union Station, 335 workers served those who took the trains east and west.
- At the east end of Main Street (682–702 Main Street), the New Brunswick Cold Storage Company plant had 50 workers.
- Maple Leaf Mills had 65 workers at their operations at 136 Mill Street, and 110 men and women distributed fruit and vegetables for Willett Fruit at 30–40 Paradise Row.
- Thorne's Hardware at the foot of King Street employed 110 people, and General Bakeries employed the same number at its Bentley Street location.

The two major establishments that were included in the survey that still exist today are the Federal Department of Transport, which then employed 110 workers to keep shipping channels well-marked, and New System Laundry, which had 130 employees. Neither employs as many workers today.

The success
of Alexander Jardine

On the back of the red-brick facade of 87 Prince William Street, the word *Jardine* is spelled out in black bricks. Most of the buildings in the area of Prince William and Water streets, which is part of the Trinity Royal Preservation District, are constructed of the same red brick. The building was owned by Alexander Jardine, who began his hardware, houseware, and shipware business in Saint John in the 1830s. Jardine was involved when the first telegraphic services came to the city in the 1840s, and in the 1850s he took out stock in the railway slated to be built from Saint John to Shediac.

When the Great Fire of 1877 destroyed his Prince William Street business, he rebuilt on the same lot. By then his son, Robert, was involved in the business with him, and they lived in a castle-like home called Craigie Lee on Westmorland Road in the east of the city. It is said this house had the first indoor bathtub in Saint John.

The fact that Alexander Jardine went to the expense of inlaying his name in the rear of his building suggests that he thought he would carry on the business for many years after the 1877 fire, but it was not to be. He died in February 1878. One account said the cause of his death was the "labour and anxiety" he experienced as he rebuilt his business. His estate was probated, and showed his wealth at $127,000 upon his death. Considering that a newspaper sold for a cent at the time, Jardine was a very wealthy man indeed!

A thirst-quenching eyesore

In 1883, to mark the centennial of Saint John's founding, the Women's Christian Temperance Union (WCTU) raised funds to have a monument erected at the head of King Street in King's Square. The monument, built to honour the Loyalist women of 1783, took the form of a public drinking fountain in keeping with the women's belief that water was the best liquid

A postcard of the King's Square WCTU monument, the so-called 'ugliest monument in Canada' in 1883

a person could imbibe. The fountain featured water spigots for dogs, horses, and people. One source noted that at the unveiling of the fountain on July 1, the members of the WCTU promised they would continue fundraising, so the monument would remain "a thing of beauty and a joy forever."

Not everyone agreed with this assessment of the fountain's appearance. The *Saint John Globe* referred to the monument as "hideous," and asked if it was a "gatepost, or a dissipated tombstone" in its tongue-in-cheek commentary. When comedian Walter Pelham came to the city in mid-July, and publicly made fun of the monument, the *Globe* commented that although the ladies' efforts were "kindly and well intentioned," Pelham's jests reflected "popular sentiment."

In spite of these comments, it was not public scorn that caused the fountain's removal. In 1963, it became so unstable that it was about to topple into traffic. It was removed to the Millidgeville Cold Mix Plant for storage. The city promised that it would eventually be erected elsewhere, but it was eventually buried in a berm of earth at the edge of Boars Head Road, where, it is presumed to repose to this day.

Let there be light!

After a full year of work, several hundred experiments, and forty-thousand pages of notes, Thomas Edison finally perfected the incandescent light bulb. His success was announced to the public in the *New York Herald* on December 21, 1879.

Saint John papers immediately picked up the story, and it was decided that a demonstration of the Edison light would be included in the celebration of the city's centennial on May 18, 1883.

In response to a request from the City's centennial committee, the Phoenix Electric Company sent engineer Arthur S. Hickley to Saint John on May 8, 1883, to prepare a demonstration of the electric light. He ran into many difficulties, as neither his wire nor his dynamo arrived as planned. But, like Edison, he persevered and on the night of May 18 at 7:20 pm, electric lights were seen glowing in Saint John—one was on King Street outside the Royal Hotel (near the corner of Germain Street, where Brunswick Square is today); another was down the hill at the A. B. Sheraton Carpet Warehouse; a third was located on Canterbury Street at the office of the *Daily Telegraph*; and the fourth lit up the post office at the corner of Prince William and Princess streets, a building that still stands today.

The seeds were sown for the electrification of the city. That took place in 1884, when a power plant capable of lighting four hundred bulbs was built on Paradise Row, in what was then the city of Portland. The next year, the streets of Carleton (Saint John West) were lit by a plant capable of running 1,800 bulbs. Saint John proper began to make the change to electric lights in 1889, using power from a plant at the corner of Smythe, Union, and Dock streets, but electrification was not completed until 1906. That was when the plant owners, the Saint John Street Railway Company, finally got control of the gas plant that had continued to provide some of the lighting on city streets.

Take me to your leader

When Ellen Kierstead was a member of the Saint John Regional Library Archives staff, she took a keen interest in compiling files on all of the mayors who served Saint John from 1785 until 1983. This collection, now further updated, is a great source for trivia about Saint John's mayors.

The first seventeen mayors (from 1785 to 1851) were appointed by the lieutenant-governor of New Brunswick. One man, William Black, did the job so well, he was appointed three times; another, Laughlin Donaldson, was appointed twice. Between 1851 and 1854, council members elected the mayor. James Olive was the last mayor chosen by appointment, and he was the first mayor elected by citizens in 1854.

Between 1854 and 2007, fifty-two individuals were elected to the position. Three were elected twice—Edward Sears in 1898 and 1906; D. Laurence Maclaren in 1936 and again in 1958; and Ernest W. Patterson in 1948 and 1952.

On September 23, 1922, Mayor H. R. McLellan was recalled from office by the citizens of Saint John because of his refusal to get on with the formation of the Saint John Power Commission, despite his promise to do so during his April campaign. He lost a subsequent election in November to G. Fred Fisher.

Five mayors have died while in office. John Robinson was the first in 1828, followed by George Barker in 1889, Frank Potts in 1926, D. Laurence Maclaren in 1958, and H. Avard Loomer in 1969.

The first female mayor was Elsie E. Wayne, who was elected in 1983 and served for ten years. She was succeeded by her deputy mayor, Tom Higgins, who served as mayor in 1994 and

1995. He was followed by Shirley McAlary, who held the position until 2004.

Two pairs of fathers and sons have served as mayor of the city. John M. Wilmot was mayor from 1833 to 1834, while his son Robert Duncan Wilmot served from 1849 to 1850. W. O. Smith was mayor from 1852 to 1853 and from 1855 to 1859. His son, A. Chipman Smith, led the city from 1874 to 1877. The younger Smith completed his term just before the Great Fire of 1877. The mayor who served the city as it was rebuilding was Sylvester Z. Earle, whose carved image can still be seen on the Chubb Building at the corner of Prince William and Princess streets.

A sketch of one of the city's most popular mayors, Simeon Jones

The lure of the lake

The Balls Lake Fishing Club traces its beginning to 1810, when George Ball was granted property deep in the woods between Mispec and the Black River Road, which included a portion of Pleasant Lake. Ball initially used the land for farming, but by the 1830s he had acquired the entire lake, and recognized its potential as a fishing spot. It was renamed Balls Lake. In 1894, forty men each invested one hundred dollars to purchase Ball's assets, including the lake. They formed the Balls Lake Fishing Club with the aim, according to their constitution, of "promoting [the] health and recreation of its members through pursuit of fishing and hunting." George McAvity was the club's first president, and William Evans was appointed as caretaker of the property.

In 1942 the club had only thirteen members, no doubt due to the number of men off to war. The fishing results varied from year to year, too, ranging from a couple hundred to almost two thousand catches. Every catch was recorded in a log, and the numbers were reviewed at the club's annual meeting. The club continues to operate quietly so that intruders do not disrupt their pristine lake. It now has forty members, who are still catching good quantities of trout from Balls Lake.

Carolling around the Christmas tree

On December 24, 1924, Saint John's first lit Christmas tree was placed in King's Square. The newly formed Power Commission of the City of Saint John placed the lights on the tree and provided the power to light them. In later years, the Saint John High School Alumni were responsible for the tree; although they are not mentioned in the media coverage from 1924, it is likely they were involved with the ceremony even at that early date, as the girls' choir from that school was the first group to sing around the newly lit community tree. Other choirs that sang that year were from the Queen

Square Methodist Church, St. David's Church, Portland Street Methodist Church, as well as a combined choir from St. James and St. John's (Stone) Church.

Mystery instrument hits the right note

Just what kind of instrument is perched upon the top of the King's Square bandstand that was donated by the City Cornet Band in 1909 has long been debated in the city. Longtime members of the St. Mary's, the City Cornet, and the Third Field Regiment bands have suggested that it may be a flugelhorn, a cornet, or an E-flat alto saxhorn; however, it is none of the above, and even the best musician could not toot a note out of the instrument. It is just a mix of metal formed into the shape of a horn of some kind.

The truth about the horn was discovered in May 1981, when it went missing. Police later found it in a gym bag in a van parked on Princess Street. The owner of the van claimed that he found the instrument in King's Square while walking his dog. The judge did not believe him, and fined him $250, and ordered the horn returned to the City of Saint John. It was carefully examined at the time, and while it was agreed it was not a real instrument, it was decided that the horn still deserved its place atop the bandstand—and it remains there to this day.

Tales from underground

Folklore has trumped truth about Howe's Caves since they were discovered in Rockwood Park in 1843 by the Oliver family, who were likely fishing for trout in the park's thirteen lakes.

The idea that a bottomless lake exists in the caves is a popular tale. Another story suggests that they are so extensive that those who enter the caves in Rockwood Park can emerge several kilometres away at Three Mile House on the East Side or at the Reversing Falls on the West Side. Another bit of folklore suggests that these caves have been explored since 1811, as this date is written on the wall of one of the deeper chambers; however, as it was written in red spray paint, it certainly must have appeared at a much later date. These stories have been denied by leading spelunkers and museum specialists, yet they persist as urban folklore in Saint John.

Quispamsis group poses in the mouth of Howe's caves

What is true is that the caves are great for beginning explorers, if they can find them. They are not on a marked trail, and it is not easy to find the unmarked path off Sandy Point Road that leads to them. But the many ropes and wires that snake through the caves' chambers prove that many explorers have found their way. Unfortunate evidence of visitors to Howe's Caves includes garbage, and broken stalactites that took centuries to form. It is believed the caves are the result of the flow of a river that worked its way through the limestone rock eons ago.

Execution of Redburn the Sailor

In Saint John, two bits of lore circulate about Charles Redburn, the sailor who stabbed Patrick Carling to death aboard the barque *Jane Hammond* on November 2, 1846. The facts of Redburn's crime are well known and undisputed. The incident took place because Redburn, the cook, who was very hungover, refused to serve Carling his breakfast. With the crew at his side, Redburn borrowed another man's knife, diverted Carling's attention by throwing greasy scalding water on him, and then stabbed him between the ribs. Redburn was tried, found guilty, and sentenced to be hanged on December 29, 1846.

One bit of lore about Redburn is that he was the first person to be hanged in the new jail on King Street East. This story stands up to scrutiny, as the five-year-old jail had never been the site of a hanging. There would not be another for eleven years. The other tale states that officials buried Redburn in the Old Burial Ground just across from the jail, despite the fact that they were officially closed. In fact, the Burial Ground wasn't closed until two years later.

During Redburn's trial, word spread around the city that he

was the son of a rich merchant, and there was quite a ground-swell of support to have his sentence commuted. This feeling was especially strong among the ladies of the community, many of whom who had formed romantic notions about the affair, perhaps due to the ideas portrayed in popular novels of the time, or because they listened to nautical songs about poor sailors who fell into crime once they left the influence of their homes and mothers. Officials ignored their protests, and Redburn was duly hanged. Three days later, the *Morning News* contained a letter he had written on the day before his execution to thank the ladies and gentlemen of Saint John who had signed the petition to save him. He did not, even then, admit his guilt.

Shaping young minds

Friedrich Froebel (1782–1852) was the German originator of Kindergarten systems, who designed building blocks that many preschool students love to play with and learn from. His ideas were championed in Saint John by Mrs. W. C. Matthews, who was the principal of the Froebel School in 1913. That year, the school's graduation ceremony was held on June 28 at St. David's Church on Sydney Street, which today is Calvary Temple. On that night, there were six graduates: Mabel Sandall, Annie Johnson, Julie Pirie, Ruth Mann, Janet Freeze, and Edith Emmerson. Well-known writer Reverend H. A. Cody presented the students' certificates at the conclusion of an evening that included demonstrations of games, finger plays, and skits that exemplified the Froebel methods of training for young minds. A copy of the program, which was donated by the Pirie family to the

New Brunswick Museum, lists Julie Pirie as having performed a story called "The Little Gray Pony." It may have been kept in the family papers as her dad, Anthony A. Pirie, was a horseshoer in North End Saint John, who surely found his daughter's story especially interesting, given his profession.

Hollywood, New Brunswick style

On August 23, 1922, a full-page advertisement in the *Saint John Globe* announced the formation of New Brunswick Films Limited by Ernest Shipman. Shipman intended to film the movie version of Frederick William Wallace's novel *Blue Water* in and around Saint John. Shipman, who had filmed six other movies in Canada, set up in the Dufferin Hotel on King Square South. He brought in screenwriter Faith Green and director David Hartford, and in October, they began shooting scenes with the film's stars, Norma Shearer, Pierre Gendron, and Jane Thomas in Chance Harbour (or Beaver Harbour, according to some accounts). Rain plagued the shoot from the start. Some storm scenes were shot indoors, using model boats in a makeshift tub at the St. Andrews Roller Rink on Charlotte Street. Other scenes were shot on the streets and in the homes of Saint John.

The film was completed in Florida. Saint Johners waited anxiously for it to appear, and finally, in January 1924, a private showing was held for investors in the city. Among them was the famed writer, H. A. Cody, whose hope that one of his own

A promotional pamphlet for Blue Water *is the only visual that remains of this early moviemaking attempt*

novels might be filmed had led him to invest two thousand dollars in the venture, all of which was lost. This was a tremendous amount of money for a clergyman to lose at the time.

Blue Water eventually played at the Imperial Theatre on April 16 and 17, 1924. The theatre was filled for the showings, and reactions to the film were positive. It also played in a few other Maritime locations, but Shipman could not get it into mainstream theatres. He realized his foray into filmmaking in Canada was over. *Blue Water* was stored in a vault in New York, but was never shown again, and like all films of the era it gradually turned to dust.

Racing on the bay

Coldbrook Park (now known as the Exhibition Park Raceway) opened in July 1930 with a modern grandstand to seat four thousand people, and stables for one hundred horses. Many of those who were there for the occasion spoke of the days when the prime race location in the city was the Courtenay Bay mud flats. They would not have attended the races at Courtenay Bay themselves, but would have heard the stories from their parents, who in turn would have heard the tales from their parents. Races at Courtenay Bay were held as far back as 1810, and continued until a track known as Moosepath Park was developed off Rothesay Avenue in the 1870s.

The following offers a description of a race day on the flats in 1845:

> The Saint John subscription races will take place on Saturday, November 22. Horses to be entered and shown on King Square, Wednesday, November 19th at 12 O'clock. The amount of the different prizes will be given as soon as subscriptions are collected. The postponement of the races from the 16th to the 22nd has been in consequence of the tides answering better on the later day. Cap. Hare, R.N., James Peters Jr., A. Edwards, J.H. Gray, T. B. Long, stewards.

A later description indicates that three races were held that day before a large number of spectators. The day was considered a holiday, and anyone who could get to the races did. The first and second races were won by Mr. Gilbert's horse, Retriever, and the third, a saddle and bridle competition, was won by Mr. McMonagle's Prize Fighter. The story noted that, "owing to excellent arrangements on the occasion no accidents or casualty occurred to mar the proceedings."

A tower of frightening faces

The tower of St. John's Church in the parish of St. Mark featuring thirty-two grotesques carved into sandstone was completed in 1829. St. John's is nicknamed the Stone Church, because it was a rarity when it was built, in part from ship's ballast in 1824, as most of the city's buildings were made of wood.

Few people have had the privilege of climbing to the top of the bell tower and seeing the grotesques up close. In fact, because they have blackened over time, few people even realize they are there, staring down over the city. When Cian Horrobin was a student guide, he loved to take visitors up into the tower. He told them that the faces, which were designed by John Cunningham, were meant to represent people who were members of the congregation at the time. No one knows for sure if Horrobin's story is true—but if it is, either the congregation members were very homely, or the stonemason was very untalented, for there is no way that the faces can be called beautiful.

If you care to see the grotesques first-hand, take a pair of binoculars and stand on Carleton Street at the corner of Wellington Row, and look up. Be sure to take someone who can steady you as you gawk, for these faces are not called grotesques for nothing.

An apple a day

The first Boy Scout troop in Saint John was formed in September 1910. During the early years, one of the movement's most innovative programs was Boy Scout Apple Day.

Eli Buyaner, funder of Apple Day, salutes Princess Elizabeth

The first Apple Day was held on January 30, 1932, when twenty-one thousand apples were sold on the streets of Saint John, generating one thousand dollars in receipts. The effort caught the attention of the Scout's national office in Ottawa, which issued a pamphlet that described the effort in the city, and featured photos of Saint John Scouts in recognizable locations such as King Street. The Scouts had visited the city's theatres and sold apples between shows, and were so courteous when visiting businesses they had been invited to come again. The pamphlet also described how the street railway company had devoted one of its cars to providing uniformed Scouts with free transportation throughout the day as they peddled their apples. The success of the campaign prompted the Scouts to undertake a second Apple Day in October 1932, and from then on, the event was held in the fall. At that time of year, the Scouts could sell New Brunswick apples, rather than more expensive imports.

A mossy money-maker

Many residents of Millidgeville are aware that an airport was once located where suburban houses now stand. The airport was built in 1928 and served the area until 1951. When digging flower beds in their backyards, some residents have run into the tarmac that famed aviators like Ruth Nichols and Amelia Earhart landed on back in the pioneering days of flight in the Maritimes.

The area would likely not have been considered usable as an airfield if the boglands, then known as the Cariboo Plains at Millidgeville, had not been drained in the 1890s so that moss could be extracted from the area. In December 1894, the *Daily Sun* carried the story of T. C. Wallace's Moss Litter Operations, located on E. H. Turnbull's Alderbrook Farm on McCoskery Road (Millidge Avenue today). The area, which had been drained into the Kennebecasis River using a frost-proof pipe, was described as having two to three metres (seven to ten feet) of accumulated moss. Turnbull, the article states, had found a way to press the water from the moss using steam power. In doing so, he had overcome the main obstacle to extracting the valued product along the Bay of Fundy, where natural drying was difficult due to damp fog.

The operation was so successful that Wallace's men were to continue the work through the winter of 1894, while he travelled south to the United States to try to generate capital to extract moss from other bogs on an even larger scale. It is not known when the extraction of moss ceased in the area, nor is it known if Wallace's venture south was a success.

Christmas wishes and warnings

One of the earliest comments about the Christmas season and its festivities to appear in a Saint John newspaper was an editorial printed in the *Saint John Morning News* on December 23, 1840. The *Morning News* advised that no paper would be published on Christmas Day, and provided readers with the following advice:

> On Monday, however, we will again throw ourselves into the hands of such of our readers as may not have died of dyspepsia during the interim. We advise abstemiousness, temperance, and plenty of exercise on Christmas-day; and as we will not have a better opportunity to express our concern for the health and happiness of our Patrons, we will conclude this paragraph by wishing them all a very Merry Christmas, a good appetite, and as much pork as they can buy for a shilling, to grease their throats for a good dinner.

Progress at the pumps

The first gas station with drive-in service at the pumps was built on Douglas Avenue at the corner of Falls View Drive in 1922. The station was so successful that it was enlarged in 1928. The owner and manager was Joseph B. Patchell, who was listed in city directories in 1919 as a returned soldier boarding in Fairville. His living arrangements remained the same for the next three years. In 1925 he listed as living at 16 Harding Street, and in 1926 at 13 Brunswick Place, just a block from the station. After the service station closed, Tim Isaac began a successful antique business in the building in 1969.

In Saint John East, the first service station that sold Red Indian fuel was built by the John Flood Company on the southeast side of the Marsh Bridge. The station was opened on

Attendant smoking at the service station at Haymarket Square

September 14, 1929, and the same Joseph Patchell was listed as its owner.

Reading between the lines of Douglas How and Ralph Costello's book *K. C.—The Biography of K. C. Irving*, the dominant player in the gasoline business today began selling gas in Buctouche and Shediac before coming to Saint John in 1925. Irving formed K. C. Irving Gas and Oil Ltd in 1927, and employed such notables as Ray Tanton and Charles Gorman as operators of his early service stations.

Hockey Night in Saint John

The Saint John Forum was built at 130–150 Main Street in the North End in 1932. The building was owned by Murray W. Long and Harry B. Tippett; they hired a well-known sportsman, Ernest A. Lamy, as the Forum's first manager. He used his National Hockey League (NHL) contacts to entice the Montreal Canadiens to hold their pre-season camp in Saint John in October 1934. One of Lamy's aces was the fact that only a few rinks in the Maritimes had artificial ice in those days. The Forum had been operating since the previous fall, and had proven itself for a full season, so Lamy was sure he could provide the great ice surface required by the professional teams.

On October 29, at the end of their 1934 camp, the Canadiens played an exhibition game against the Boston Bruins. During the pre-season the following year the Canadiens once again played Boston in Saint John, but this time it was the Bruins who were holding their training camp at the Forum. The following October, neither team held its training camp in Saint John, but exhibition games between the Bruins and the Canadiens and the Maroons of Montreal did take place at the Forum. The players stayed at the leading hotel in the city, the Admiral Beatty, and competed for what was called the Admiral Beatty Cup.

Though the players praised the ice as the best they had ever skated on, after 1936 no further NHL games were noted in papers of the era.

Mysterious marble man

A marble statue on the Farren plot at St. Joseph's Cemetery is one of the few human figures depicted in stone to be found in Saint John's dozen or so cemeteries. It is natural to assume that the statue represents the gentleman who is buried there, but there is no proof that is the case.

Patrick Farren, Esquire, arrived in Saint John in 1854 or 1855. According to Peter Murphy, who has a vast knowledge of Irish history, Farren married Brigit Kane on November 3, 1859, and the couple operated a grocery and liquor business on Britain Street in the south end of Saint John. They had four children, and the stories of the deaths of two of their sea-going sons-in-law are noted on the monument. Murphy says the stone figure may represent one of the two sea captains, or it may simply be a factory-produced statue and not depict anyone buried there.

Radio heard through the Bamboo Curtain

In tribute to her husband, Senator Clarence V. Emerson, Francis Emerson made a series of radio programs with CFBC, followed by a series of television programs with CHSJ. The television series began in the summer of 1970, and featured Scottish baritone Niven Miller. The television program spread far beyond Saint John, and was eventually taped in colour in Ontario and shown across North America. The radio program was heard across the Pacific Ocean in China, where it was played beyond the so-called Bamboo Curtain. As a result Francis Emerson received the Asia Peace Award in New York in 1972.

Niven Miller continued to sing and teach in his native Scotland, and has not been in Canada for many years; however, those with turntables can still hear him, for six of the records he made as part of the tribute to Senator Emerson are available at the Saint John Regional Library.

Pantaloons, petticoats, and pews

We think of our ancestors as being very conservative, and indeed they were—but sometimes, practical considerations forced them to be a bit less reserved. In 1838 there was very little open space available in the city centre where

The ornate fence fronting Trinity Church that the Saint John ladies used to dry their petticoats

citizens could dry their laundry. There was, however, a nice iron rail fence around Trinity Church right in the heart of downtown, where the vestry permitted laundresses who washed clothes for various noblemen and ladies to hang their laundry to dry.

This practice displeased one man, who wrote a letter to the editor using the pen name "Pew Holder, middle aisle." He asked the paper to "please inform the church wardens and vestrymen of Trinity Church that the pew owners and occupiers request that they will in future direct their several laundresses to carry their old pantaloons, shirts, drawers, petticoats, etc, to the respective drying grounds of each vestryman for the purpose of public exhibition, instead of parading their offensive traps on the front railing and steps leading to Trinity Church on Germain Street." The writer pointed out that St. Andrew's Kirk and the Methodist Chapel did not permit "such offensive articles" to be exhibited.

North ender Nicholson hits the big leagues

North ender Neil Nicholson grew up playing hockey on a backyard rink his father flooded at their Victoria Street home, and became the first native Saint Johner to play in the National Hockey League. Neil's brother David says Neil got his start in minor hockey on the surface of the old Saint John Forum on Main Street, and later played in the Lord Beaverbrook Rink that David now manages, which is also on Main Street.

Neil's first professional stints were with the Oakland Seals in 1969 and 1970, and the Providence Reds in 1971 and 1972. During the 1972–73 season he was called up to the NHL and played thirty games with the New York Islanders, and the following season he played a further eight games. After three years back in the Central Hockey League with Fort Worth, he played his final game in the NHL during the 1977–78 season. In total he played thirty-nine games in the NHL, and had three goals and one assist. After his career in North America ended, Neil spent nine years playing hockey in Europe, primarily in Switzerland. He now travels through the Maritimes working for McCann Equipment. Although his professional playing days have come to an end, Neil's interest in hockey has not waned.

No girls allowed

In 1935, the Kiwanis Club of Saint John, concerned with the adequacy of recreational facilities for boys in the city's North End, took over the operation of the Shamrock Grounds on Lansdowne Avenue. The area became known as the K Grounds.

By 1938, the Kiwanis Club reported that they had succeeded in building a track that was "recognized as the best in Eastern Canada, and one of the best throughout the country." The report also stated that new playground facilities at the K Grounds were better than any others in the city of Saint John.

The club was concerned with one aspect of the operations of the grounds. They informed city council that girls had increasingly begun to use the grounds, but noted that "toilet and other arrangements were not provided for the girls, nor has there been any woman appointed to supervise the work of such girls." The Kiwanis Club felt that under the circumstances, the presence of girls on K Grounds created a "definite hazard." They recommended that "no girls be permitted on the Grounds until all safeguards in proper facilities and supervision [had] been provided." And so no girls were allowed…at least until the improvements were made.

What's in a (misspelled) name?

When Riverview Memorial Park on Douglas Avenue was under development at the beginning of the twentieth century several other names were considered for the area. Parraduburg was one of five proposed names for the park, which was created to honour those who had served in the Boer War. A committee of citizens had secured six parcels of land at 277 Douglas Avenue, between the New Brunswick Museum and the Gregory House (now the Grews) for the project. The group chose Parraduburg as a possibility, as it was the site of a famed battle that men from Saint John fought in during the war in South Africa; however, they had spelt the name incorrectly. The proper spelling is Paardeberg, so it is just as well that it wasn't chosen when the committee placed their suggestions for the name of the park before the public.

Of the five options, Outlook received 6 votes, La Tour received 13, Memorial got 43, Parraduburg received 125 votes, and the winner, Riverview, took 234 votes. The White Bronze Company erected a monument at edge of the embankment overlooking Marble Cove at a cost of $1,400. Citizens were invited to dump their refuse beyond the statue in order to build up the hill and enlarge the usable parkland on the river side of the property. Imagine that happening today!

Ron Zelward's Tiny Town

On a bluff not far from the Saint John Airport, at 7 Lomond Drive, is Ron Zelward's Tiny Town, an attraction that is free to the public, and draws hundreds of curious visitors travelling on Highway 820 to Upham.

Ron's miniature village got its start because of a pet squirrel the family called Peter. He would sit on Ron's shoulder and take peanuts right out of his mouth and pockets. Ron's wife, Lorna, suggested that Peter needed a house to live in, and after some thought, Ron built the squirrel a little blue bungalow.

After building Peter's house, Ron constructed a church, schoolhouse, fire station, lighthouse, bar, bank, grocery store, and fitness centre. He also built an airport, and at his wife's suggestion, a replica of the arena where her favourite hockey team, the Toronto Maple Leafs, plays. Tiny Town has now grown to thirty-five scale model houses and businesses on the Zelward property. The results of many hours spent in Ron's workshop throughout the

Ron Zelward at Tiny Town in 2005

winter are available for viewing from spring through fall. Ron's visitors' book shows that folks from one end of the country to the other have found and enjoyed Tiny Town.

Lights and lines

In July 1929 the first stoplight in the province of New Brunswick was installed at the corner of Union and Charlotte streets in uptown Saint John—and it didn't cost taxpayers a single cent. The Brilliant Electric Company had entered into an agreement with the city to pay for this set of lights, as well as twenty-three others in Saint John, in exchange for the rights to advertise various products on the overhead signals. In addition, the company agreed to pay the City five dollars per year for each advertisement, and to set up a showroom and traffic light factory in the city that would employ up to 150 people.

Another traffic innovation we take for granted today is the white line. The first in the province also appeared in Saint John in 1929. After Officer Edward Sowery had a near miss on his motorcycle while making a dangerous *S* turn on Rothesay Avenue under the Brookville railway overpass, he painted a white line on the centre of the roadway, and ordered drivers to stay on their own side of the line or face a fine.

"Red Rose Tea is Good Tea"

T H. Estabrooks's tea plant, built in 1903, still stands at .39–45 Mill Street in Saint John, and is used as an office complex in the city centre. Estabrooks's beautiful home at 112 Mount Pleasant Avenue, built in 1904, is known as the Red Rose Mansion, and until recently was a bed and breakfast.

Estabrooks's tea lives on, too, and remains a favourite in Maritime kitchens and with tea drinkers across the nation. In his heyday, Estabrooks had Canadian plants and warehouses in Montreal, Toronto, Edmonton, Calgary, St. John's, and in the United States at Houlton and Portland in Maine. It mattered not where the tea was sold, it was always sold under the same motto: "Red Rose Tea is Good Tea." It is said Estabrooks developed the slogan after hearing a lady in a general store in Saint John ask the grocer for "some of that good Red Rose tea." In 1932 he sold his company to Brooke Bond and Company, which continued to operate much as he had. Estabrooks died in 1945. The plant was sold to Unilever in 1984 and they closed tea operations in 1988.

Saint John's Father
of Confederation

The statue of Sir Samuel Leonard Tilley stands proudly in King's Square, looking down King Street to the corner of Germain Street, a place he crossed a thousand times during his sixty-five years in Saint John. Tilley walked the route on his way to services at St. John's (Stone) Church at the end of Wellington Row. Why he walked from his home, Carleton House at 223 Germain, past Trinity Church to the Stone Church is not known, for both are Anglican churches.

It was Tilley who suggested to Prime Minister Sir John A. Macdonald that the country be named the Dominion of Canada. While engaged in his daily scripture reading, Tilley was inspired by the following section from Psalm 72:8: "He shall have dominion also from sea to sea and from the river unto the end of the earth." The idea appealed to Macdonald, and he saw that the title was adopted.

When Tilley died at three o'clock in the morning on June 25, 1896, his parting words were: "I can go to sleep now. New Brunswick has done well." He was still passionately interested in the Conservative Party he had supported. Tilley died without knowing that although his party had done well in New Brunswick, it had gone down in defeat in the general election beyond the borders of his beloved province.

The statue of Tilley, designed by famed Montreal sculptor Phillippe Hebert, was cast in France, and unveiled on September 8, 1910, in King's Square. In addition his impressive gravestone at Fernhill Cemetery is still visited by many who are interested in political matters. Each July 1, dozens of citizens come to the cemetery to honour Tilley and another Father of Confederation, William Henry Steeves. Fernhill is the only cemetery in Canada where two Fathers of Confederation are buried.

Salvation Army at Sabaskastaggan Creek

Sabaskastaggan Creek is the Mi'kmaq name for Marsh Creek, which means "a beaver trench nearly goes through." When the Mi'kmaq first encountered the creek, there were likely many beaver channels there. There may still be beaver living in the upper portion of the creek above Glen Falls in the hills behind the Mackay Highway, where the water is pristine.

When the Salvation Army arrived in Saint John and opened its first barracks in 1885, the creek was polluted, and rum sellers were the main inhabitants of the houses on its banks. The organization could not do anything about the pollution in the water, but felt it could offer a better way of life to those living at Marsh Bridge, as reported in its magazine, *The War Cry*. The article, reprinted in the *Saint John Globe* on April 7, 1888, under the heading "Marsh Creek Bridge for Jesus," described the group's plan to "bombard two rum shops at the Marsh Bridge...and to tear the devil's kingdom right down." The outcome of this particular foray is unknown. The Salvation Army's work continued to expand, and its founder, General William Booth, visited the group's citadel on Charlotte Street in Saint John when it was completed in 1907. The work of the organization on behalf of the poor and disenfranchised continues unabated to this day.

Navy Island Bridge— a century in the making

Beginning in 1857, various plans were put forth to build a second bridge across Saint John Harbour, using Navy Island as its western anchor. The idea was first proposed by Kilby Reynolds, who built the original suspension bridge at the Reversing Falls in 1853. Reynolds' plan would have affected some council members' properties, and they managed to have the idea quashed.

The present-day Harbour Bridge which took almost a century from its first proposal to complete

As time passed, citizens of North End (Portland) and Saint John West began to feel more and more alienated from the city. When the city proper and Portland amalgamated in 1889, the ire of the west siders was so great they decided to form a city of their own. This got council's attention, and they hired engineer F. W. Holt to prepare plans for a harbour bridge that would link the centre of town to the business heart of Saint John West on Union Street. The designs had to incorporate a mid-channel drawbridge that would allow vessels to pass up and down the Straight Shore. Holt conducted soundings to determine the depth of the water, and came up with four possible bridge designs. Holt's work was all for naught as none of his plans went ahead. Other proposals were completed in 1909, 1929, and 1952. Finally, the Saint John Harbour Bridge was constructed and opened on August 17, 1968. The bridge cost eighteen million dollars, and is still in use today.

Royal Oaks in Rockwood Park?

The oak trees that thrive in Rockwood Park are often said to have grown from acorns brought to the area by a sea captain who lived on Mount Pleasant Avenue. Because some people have suggested that the acorns may have come from Buckingham Palace, the trees are known as "royal oaks." The story can't be proven, but it has been told for decades, and may hold a grain of truth.

The park's horticultural gardens are built on soil that came into the port as ballast. Many of the swampy depressions around Lily Lake were also filled in with ballast from ships coming to the port from England. It is very possible that there may have been acorns in the earth. For example, at the roadside in Perth-Andover stands a huge white oak, which was planted in 1887 by Senator and Mrs. George Baird to mark Queen Victoria's Golden Jubilee. That oak was brought to the area from the grounds of Windsor Castle. So the dwarf oaks that grow so profusely on Hemlock Hill in Rockwood Park may too be descendents of royal oaks planted after the park began to develop in 1894.

A home where the buffalo roam

When Rockwood Park was redeveloped for the city of Saint John's marking of the nation's centennial in 1967, a demonstration farm was added to the attractions at the 970-hectare (2,400-acre) site. Overseen by Doug and Muriel Fordham, the farm was home to chickens, ducks, horses, cows, and sheep, and a wolf, bear, and deer also lived on the farm. Certainly the most unusual critters in the park were a pair of buffalo given by the Halton Region Conservation Authority in Ontario. The buffalo named Doug arrived at the farm in 1969, while the other, Muriel, arrived in 1972.

Doug and Muriel, the humans, took special interest in their namesakes. Buffalo are natural roamers, and on the night of Wednesday, July 19, 1973, Doug got loose. He travelled as far as Hawthorne Avenue, where the Thibodeau family heard him tearing up trees and eating flowers on their property. At one point they thought the animal might charge through their window. Police were called, and fearing that the two-thousand-pound animal might go on a rampage, they shot him. There was only one tranquilizer gun in the province at the time, and the police decided they could not wait for it to be sent to Saint John from Fredericton. Mayor Bob Lockhart and Police Chief Harry McKay both said they regretted the shooting, but commented that people's lives had to take priority over a buffalo's life. Muriel must have missed Doug very much, for she died less than six months later of heart failure.

A winter wonder

Stella Maris Church at the corner of Bayside Drive and Park Avenue is one of many buildings constructed by the venerable John Flood and Company in and around Saint John. Many people do not know the church's name means "star of the sea," and many also do not know that the building of the church in 1924 proved once and for all that winter construction work was possible and profitable. It seems that no previous church, or other significant stone structure, had been built during winter; in a newspaper account of the project, George Flood stated that a "great many people were skeptical as to the feasibility of building during the winter months."

He further stated that "great improvements in the mode of protecting the building materials from the wintry blasts and danger of freezing" would allow winter work to carry on. He also said that these improvements had meant an increase in the amount of available work for masons and other labourers. The project's payroll amounted to $1,700 per week, as the 39-by-17-metre (127-by-55-foot) structure was raised overlooking the Courtenay Bay mud flats. Though the original plan included a 40-metre-high (130-foot-high) tower with a spire on the right side of the building, the spire portion was not completed, and the base of the tower, which is visible in old photos, has subsequently been removed. The main body of the Gothic-style building is still intact, and the church continues to serve Catholics of the area.

The word on the street

When the Loyalists settled Saint John, Sydney Street was considered the outer edge of the city. As was customary at the time, the Old Burial Ground was established outside the city boundaries in an effort to keep communicable diseases as far from the general public as possible. When housing was built in the area east of Sydney Street, and streets were extended from the west side of the street, the extensions did not always retain the original street names. For example, the extension of King Street beyond King's Square, which is known today as King Street East, was known then as Great George Street. The extension of Princess Street was called St. George's Street, Duke Street became Morris Street, and St. James Street's extension was Stormont Street.

A similar situation exists in downtown Saint John today. Germain Street, for example, becomes Wellington Row beyond Union Street, and Chipman Hill becomes Hazen Avenue on the other side of Union. Union Street is sometimes said to have been

King Street as it appeared before the Great Saint John Fire of 1877

given its name because it was the boundary between Portland and Saint John when the two cities amalgamated in 1889; however, City Road was the boundary between the two areas, and the name Union Street was in use long before amalgamation.

Loyalist Stone
loved and loathed

For almost one hundred years, a commemorative rock has stood overlooking Market Slip, which is traditionally thought of as the location where the city's Loyalist founders landed. Initially, the rock sat in a triangular grass plot that separated traffic lanes at the foot of King Street, but when Market Square opened in 1983, roads were realigned, the grass was removed, and the monument was moved closer to the harbour. It is possible that the rock now stands exactly where the landing took place, as Dock Street and Water Street were, at one time, right on the shoreline of the harbour.

The monument was not a hit with all citizens when it was first placed in Market Square. In a letter to the editor in the *Saint John Globe* on December 15, 1923, a writer identified as "Grace and Dignity," agreed with the *Globe*'s criticism of the "unsightly memorial." The writer referred to the Loyalists as "heroic and faithful pioneers" who would "gaze with dismay at such a monstrosity." Today the monument is considered one of Saint John's most sacred spots. Visitors who arrive at the nearby cruise ship terminal are shown the rock, as are school children visiting the area. The children refer to the rock as the dinosaur egg.

Thomson's ark

George Thomson came to Saint John from Scotland in 1816 to sell potatoes, as they were scarce in the city in a year when some said there was no summer. Despite the weather, he liked the new world and the opportunities it presented, so he stayed in New Brunswick. He made a fortune building vessels along the Fundy shore, many of which were sold in England, Ireland, and Scotland. He held an official government position related to the removal of ballast from ships in Saint John Harbour.

Just a few years before his death in 1841 Thomson built a lavish ark for his home at his shipyard near Fort La Tour. The ark's base was the *Daedalus*, a 396-ton ship that he had built in 1835 for Robert Rankine. The *Daedalus* had run into some difficulty, and was a derelict in Saint John Harbour when Thomson got it. He decorated it extravagantly. There were folding doors between the rooms for privacy, silver chandeliers for light, and imported silverware and china to be used at grand banquets. The ark even featured a library with a wide variety of paintings and plants. Frances Helyar's song about the ark sums up the elaborate project quite nicely: "It was all designed to please, to give George Thomson and his friends a carefree life of ease."

George wasn't able to enjoy the ark for long. He died in 1841 while trying to raise the *Wallace*, a ship he'd built that had been stranded on the Murr Ledges off Grand Manan only months after being launched. Saint Johners didn't enjoy the ark for long either, as it burnt in a New Year's Eve fire that was reported in the *Morning News* on January 1, 1847.

Art for everyday people

Hampton woodcarver John Hooper is well represented in Saint John; in fact, the city has more of his work than anywhere else in Canada.

Hundreds of thousands of people have had their picture taken at his most visible work, the 1983 *Timepiece*, at the east entrance to Market Square. *Timepiece* will be joined by the figures in Hooper's *People Waiting* sculpture, which is now owned by the City of Saint John. *People Waiting* was originally purchased by Canada Post, and stood at the Main Post Office on Rothesay Avenue until 2004, when the federal agency decided it was not in the "art business." The sculpture will be moved to a permanent outdoor location at St. Andrew's Square, foot of King, within view of the famed *Timepiece*.

There is some concern that the sculptures will not stand up to the elements, and that they may be vandalized. This happened with another sculpture, the *Security Guard*, commissioned for the west entrance of Market Square. The guard carried a two-way radio, and as a representative of the law, so to speak, he was subject to regular thrashings by passersby. As no such damage was ever inflicted on the adjacent cluster of carvings of shoppers, a plan was hatched to change the guard's walkie-talkie to a bunch of flowers. This has ended the acts of aggression the poor guard suffered.

Hooper, a peace-loving man whose portrayals of ordinary people doing ordinary things are so calming, would be pleased with the solution. The fact that *People Waiting* is joining his other downtown sculptures and will continue to delight Saint Johners and visitors would also please the artist.

Take to the air from Turnbull Field

The Saint John Airport (officially called Turnbull Field, and sometimes called Clover Valley) on Loch Lomond Road saw its first commercial flight arrive at 10:23 am on December 30, 1951, when Captain Fraser Marshall brought a Douglas DC-3 Skyliner

The first management and maintenance crew at Saint John Airport. From left to right, Ed Maloney, Don Cruickshank, Ernie Stewart, Stuart MacGregor, Harry Smith, Harold Titus, and Glendon Jones

owned by Trans-Canada Airlines in for a "flawless landing."

The plane landed on the newly-built field on the eastern out-skirts of Saint John a day earlier than expected, and the airport was still being finished as the landing took place. Glendon Jones, a member of the maintenance crew, described the group as hard-working. His work at the airport began as he helped clear the land. He recalled "chopping the trees with an axe...no chainsaws in those days, just axes and sometime, a crosscut saw."

Jones could not recall why that particular location was chosen for the airport, so he could not confirm a well-known anecdote that Clover Valley was selected because it was the least foggy location in Saint John, but that once the land was cleared the area became one of the foggier spots in the city. Certainly a curious thing, you will agree.

Along the River

Beginning in 1858 along the Kennebecasis River and in 1869 along the St. John River, railways running from Saint John allowed easy access to the countryside surrounding both rivers, and made it possible for residents to leave the city in summer and enjoy warmer weather and cleaner air in the country. Until the mid-1960s, these areas remained primarily farmland with scattered cottages, except for Rothesay, where there were a number of year-round residences and two well-established schools, Netherwood and Rothesay Collegiate.

Although no one saw it coming, in the late 1960s new housing began to be built on what had been prime farmland. It was cheaper than land in Saint John, rock did not have to be blasted away before building could take place, and taxes were low as there were no services to be paid for…initially. As growth continued, there was soon a need for schools, churches, shops, and the other amenities of modern life. This section explores some of the curiosities of the riverside communities from the earliest times to the present.

Everybody who's anybody

"Rothesay Park is likely to become a favourite summer resort for St John people who desire to live in the country during the summer months," stated a news story, accompanied by a map showing how the land between the Green (Common) and the Kennebecasis River was being developed in the early 1900s.

The owners of the Rothesay Park lots were well-known Saint Johners at the turn of the twentieth century. The list included insurance executive and real estate developer David Russell Jack, who died in 1914; George A. Hetherington, administrator of the Provincial Hospital from 1896 to 1903; the family of politician Samuel Leonard Tilley (who died in 1896), including Lady Alice Tilley, his widow, and L. P. D. Tilley, his son, who later became premier of the province; mercantile giant F. W. Daniels; and well-known citizens like Reverend John deSoyres, Justice Burbridge, and James Hannay.

A cottage in Rothesay as depicted in a turn-of-the-century postcard

Village of Westfield's last act

When Westfield and Grand Bay amalgamated at the beginning of 1998, the village of Westfield decided to erect a monument to mark one of the most catastrophic events in the two-hundred-year history of the area. The forest fire of August 6, 1921, devastated hundreds of acres across much of southern New Brunswick, and when it finally reached Westfield, it destroyed fifty-five homes and cottages. There were no deaths, though for years following the fire, many stories of close calls were shared. The monument was placed at Ononette at the corner of Nerepis and Old Nerepis roads.

Forgotten graves

When Gerry and Susie Gigou moved to Central Avenue in Epworth Park in the early 1950s, there were no permanent residents, only cottagers. It didn't bother Gerry at all that his cottage stood opposite an early settlement graveyard, and he decided to fix up the cottage and make it a permanent home for his growing family. Many others did the same and over the next fifty years almost all of the cottages were converted to allow year-round living. From time to time, Gerry and Susie would do a little work to neaten up the six-by-six-metre (nineteen-by-nineteen-foot) graveyard, and each time they did, they wondered why the descendants of the people who were buried there had not taken any interest in those who had gone before them.

The couple asked around and learned that there may have

been as many as a dozen people interred in the plot. Although there were no stones, they learned that the deceased could be John, Mary, and William Hayter, Walter Bigger, and perhaps a member of the Kirtley family, who were known to have been the first settlers in the area. The press interviewed Gerry about the matter a couple of times, but nobody ever stepped forward with more information. As they grew older Gerry and Susie had to move to more manageable living quarters in the city, and when they left their old home, one of their regrets was that the Epworth Park Cemetery was still unkempt and unmarked. Both have since died, but neither is buried at the cemetery they lived near for so long.

A fine balance

The secret behind a gravity-defying boulder on Gondola Point Road was revealed by Gerald Thompson. The granite boulder sits atop a larger rock, appearing to lean out at an impossible angle. Thompson says that Bruce McCully unearthed the larger rock some years back when a sewage system was being installed on his property. Rather than have it removed, he decided to create a conversation piece by balancing a smaller rock on top of it. The smaller rock was often knocked off by passersby, so Bruce drilled holes in both rocks, and installed an iron pin to make the astonishing balancing act permanent. Small fry often ask how it works, and Bruce informs them that it took a lot of crazy glue to accomplish the task.

Westfield's new links

Two rounds of golf on a completely redesigned course marked the official opening of the new Westfield Golf and Country Club on June 3, 1932. The official men's foursome consisted of A. B. Gilbert, the club's president; H.C. Grout, an honoured guest and former vice-president; club member Frank J. Likely; and professional golfer Harry Mealey. The first mixed foursome was made up of W. D. Foster, Mr. and Mrs. C. A. Beatteay, and Mrs. Philip Nase.

In the evening, a seven-course dinner was served in the new clubhouse, built to replace the previous clubhouse, which was constructed in 1919. The new building boasted a large lounge with a stone fireplace, a sun porch, a men's locker room upstairs, and a ladies' locker room downstairs. A dining room was added in the late 1960s, but just as the 1977 season was about to get underway it, along with the nearby pro shop, was levelled by flames. The current clubhouse, the third built on the site, was constructed following the fire, and officially opened in July 1978.

A bubbly solution

It was the winter of 1959 when an experiment to keep the Gondola Point Channel free of ice was first attempted. Air was bubbled up from lines laid on the floor of the Kennebecasis River along the ferry's usual route. At that time only one ferry made the crossing, so it was more difficult to prevent the channel from freezing during the night, when service was limited.

A cable ferry at Gondola Point, New Brunswick

A brand new town with an arena to match

Reports about the April 26, 1983, opening of the Quispamsis Arena quoted architect Blair Roma as saying it was the most modern arena in the province. He based his claim on several innovations that arena users may not have noticed, including "state of the art sodium lights;" Saint John Arena's mercury vapour lights used 50 percent more energy, he noted. Other innovations included nine miles of plastic, rather than metal, pipes to carry the refrigerant, which eliminated the possibility that the pipes may rust; and a secondary hot water heating system under the continuous pour concrete slab to prevent the soil beneath from freezing.

The arena opened just a few months after the village of Quispamsis was granted official town status on January 1, 1983, at which time the population was stated as 6,050. Town manager Donald Scott noted that a sign at Highway 1 that read "Welcome to Quispamsis, the largest village in Atlantic Canada," could be painted over. Scott also said that citizens of Rothesay would no longer be able to "rub people's noses" in the fact that it was a town, while Quispamsis was not. "We will become more than an equal partner," he was quoted as saying.

Cows on the Common

The Rothesay Common is now a very nice park, but until the 1930s it was used by cows as much as people. According to a neighbour, Tim Ellis, the Common "was where Arthur Kennedy had his cows taken every day for years. They would be driven up the road by Walter Wright from down by the station, past the school, and spend the day foraging on what was essentially swampland." The cows would wade into a brook that ran through the middle of the grounds, and by the time the men came to get them at night, they would be "black with mud," Ellis laughed.

Ellis said that after the area was spruced up and made into a place for people, patriotic fairs that became a highlight of summer were staged there. The fair's attractions included an old fellow in a tent who would share the secret of whittling for a quarter. "His secret was, 'never whittle towards you,'" Ellis laughed. Another attraction was a Native woman named Nellie Frances, who told fortunes for a quarter. One year a government representative arrived at the fair to shut down a game of crown and anchor, as it was considered gambling. Ellis guesses that Rothesay may just have been on the "wrong side of the government at the time."

Fair trade

Everyone knows that New York was bought from the Natives for twenty-four dollars in 1626, but the tale of how Darlings Island in the Kennebecasis Valley was bought for a similar sum sometime after 1770 is not as well known. A trader from Marblehead, Massachusetts, named Benjamin Darling owned property at Yarmouth, Nova Scotia, but wanted to expand his trading operations up the Fundy coast. His explorations led him to an island that was home to an established native encampment in the Kennebecasis at the mouth of the Hammond River. Darling bartered with the chief, who reluctantly sold him the property that became known as Darlings Island. According to historian W. O. Raymond, the price Darling paid for the island included "two bushels of corn, one barrel of flour, a grindstone, some powder and shot, and sundry knives, hatchets, and other implements." Some of the items he used for payment would have introduced the Natives to new innovations; Darling might be compared to a trader who today would use the latest computer as a tool for barter. Darling built a comfortable home on the island and maintained good relations with the First Nations people throughout his life.

"A spa for the soul"

When the Villa Madonna Retreat House at Renforth held its first retreat on July 10, 1931, a strictly Roman Catholic crowd attended. The building, which was conceived by Bishop LeBlanc, was one hundred feet long, and had room for thirty-seven guests. It was intended to operate only in summer. The Sisters of Charity were involved almost from the time of the retreat house's opening, and the group continued its interest until 1958. During their tenure, a winding path with the story of Christ's last days, known as the stations of the cross, was added to the woods behind the retreat house. Bishop Bray and the Catholic Community Club carried out the work on this woodsy path of prayer.

The Holy Cross Fathers took over the operation of the house in 1958. By then, the facility had been winterized. They added a chapel in 1961. In 1992, over half a million dollars were invested to modernize the Villa Madonna. Today, people of all faiths enjoy a variety of sacred and secular programs at the retreat house. Visitors come from around the world to study, enjoy fine food, wander the woodland paths, and get in touch with their inner selves at what has been called a "spa for the soul."

Laughin' Louie

Louie Morris, a Native from Shubenacadie, Nova Scotia, wandered widely in New Brunswick, from Westmorland County to Charlotte County, but he seemed to prefer the Kennebecasis Valley before suburbanization began in the area in the 1960s.

In an undated copy of the *Kings County Record*, Rothesay resident and prolific writer of letters to the editor Warren Searle shared his memories of Louie. When Searle was a young man, Louie startled him greatly by sneaking up and giving him a

The wide ranging Laughin' Louie may have visited this First Nations family depicted at Westfield in 1903.

great bear hug, but he soon learned that Louie was as harmless as a flea.

If Louie was hungry and knew of a house where a meal might be had, he just walked in, sat down, and expected to be fed. In return, he would offer a woven basket, an axe handle, or a toy bow and arrow for a child. He would also chop firewood for older people. Searle noted that Louie loved jokes—his deep, long laugh would begin well before the punchline, which is how he got the nickname Laughin' Louie.

Louie seldom stayed in one place for long. Some said he lived in a rustic shack atop Maple Mountain, while others remembered him staying in a culvert under the tracks at Model Farm Road, and still others said he stayed at a camp close to where Sobeys is today. Though Louie, one of the characters that once made life so interesting, is no longer with us, his memory is still very much alive in the Kennebecasis Valley.

Major tribute
to Hammond River

The Hammond River flows out of the hills behind Hampton, and into the Kennebecasis River through a marsh at Darlings Island. It is as pristine a river as can be found in the world today, and is a favourite with fishermen, canoeists, swimmers, and photographers. Its beauty has inspired poets and musicians, including Doug Major.

Doug came to Canada from England in the early 1940s, as a musician and musical director with Canadian Military Bands. He settled in Saint John in the late 1940s, and became organist and choirmaster at St. Paul's (Valley) Church, and associate director of both the Saint John Symphony and the Carriden Choir. Eventually he also worked with music students in Saint John's schools. He wrote many pieces of music for these groups, including a full libretto about the Loyalists to mark Canada's centennial.

Doug's daughter, Jude, says he fell in love with picturesque New Brunswick, and was always writing poems about its history and beauty. His interest turned to folk music in the early 1960s, as his teaching and conducting duties slowed. In all, he wrote a dozen pieces in a series he called *Songs of New Brunswick*. Many of these folksy pieces were sung and recorded in 1966 by a very tight folk group at the University of New Brunswick known as the Henchmen.

Doug called the eighth song in his series "Strange Names," and it included references to the Kennebecasis River and the Nauwigewauk area. Jude says Doug had a special place in his heart for the Hammond River, and it shows in this evocative piece titled "Hammond River:"

> Down in yonder sunny valley, where the fragrant pine
>   trees grow,
> Quiet runs the Hammond River, soft the murm'ring
>   breezes blow;
> On its banks the scented cedars, shade the gently flowing
>   stream,
> Ever shall its transient beauty, haunt my mem'ry and my
>   dreams.
>
> There are many other rivers, shaded banks and cedar
>   trees;
> There are many quiet valleys clothed with music of the
>   bees.
> Lilac bush and honeysuckle, stately poplars, rustling
>   leaves;
> But the waters of the Hammond haunt my mem'ries and
>   my dreams.

A simple question—Nauwigewauk?

Julie Brook gave tours of the Darlings Island Marshes for a number of years, and to augment the beauty of the marsh, and sightings of osprey, eagles, muskrats, and beavers, she would tell stories of the cottagers, canoeists, fishermen, and duck hunters, who shared the marsh with her. The story of how the Nauwigewauk got its name was one of Julie's favourites.

According to Alan Rayburn's *Geographical Names of New Brunswick*, the Maliseet called the Hammond River Nauwigewauk, and the name was selected for the railway station by the commissioners of the European and North American Railway in 1858. Neither Rayburn nor Bill Hamilton, the author of *Place Names of Atlantic Canada*, could say for certain what the word meant to the Maliseet.

But Julie Brook knows what Nauwigewauk means. According to Julie, a long time ago a Native family tried to cross the marsh from Pickwauket to Frost Mountain to what was then known as Ossekeag, now called Hampton. The wife told her husband that the ice on the marsh's surface was not strong enough to hold them, and that they should take the long way around. The distance around the end of the marsh was about eight to ten kilometres (five or six miles), compared to the shortcut across, which would be less than a mile. Her husband decided he would cross the ice anyway, so with the papoose on her back the Native woman struck out, taking the long way.

When she reached Hampton, her husband still had not arrived, even though he had taken the shortcut. In fact, he had fallen through the ice. When he swam ashore he found his wife waiting patiently for him. As he climbed out of the cold water, she said to him, "Now would you walk?" That, according to Julie, is how Nauwigewauk got its name.

Becoming Rothesay

Among the papers of Elizabeth Walker Thomson, 1854–1942, was a handwritten account of Rothesay as it was when the railway came to the area on June 1, 1858. At that time the entire area was known as Kennebecasis, and the railway station, at first, took that name, too.

The European and North American Railway had bought a large tract of land from Elizabeth's father, Robert Thomson, and a section of the track that led to the station was known as Thomson's Curve. Following a visit to the area by the Prince of Wales (once the Duke of Saxony, Cornwall, and Rothesay, and later Edward VII) Robert Thomson suggested the railway station, and thus the town, be renamed Rothesay. Elizabeth Thomson was undoubtedly very proud of this fact.

Eleanor Jones's Quiz-pamsis

In 1983, Eleanor Jones, unofficial historian of the town of Quispamsis, was asked to prepare a quiz on the town she had lived in for forty years. Eleanor had watched the population grow from only 200 to 6,022, and she had seen the countryside change from farmland with a few cottagers, to a town spread over an area of thirty-six square kilometres. Some of Eleanor's questions might stump current residents:

Who is Ritchie Lake named after?
Ritchie Lake was the sumptuous summer resort of the

Honourable William Johnstone Ritchie, who rose from being a lawyer in Saint John to the position of Canada's chief justice. He lived from 1813 to 1892. He purchased a thousand acres around the little lake in about 1855, about the same time that it became accessible by rail. Ritchie called his estate Kawatcoose, replacing the Maliseet name, Quispamsis, which meant little lake.

Who had the title of unofficial first mayor of Quispamsis?

The unofficial first mayor of Quispamsis was Henry MacEachern, who died in 1978 at the age of eighty-six. MacEachern was a tireless promoter of the area, who visited hundreds of children in their homes dressed as Santa Claus spreading goodwill in the community.

Where was Quispamsis's first church?

The first church in Quispamsis was St. Augustine's Anglican on Pettingill Road, built in 1894. The church is still active today.

Miss Canada's Quispamsis connection

The first Miss Canada ever chosen was Saint John's own Winifred Blair who competed against young women from across the country at the competition in February 1923 in Montreal. After winning, Winifred was promised many prizes, including the chance to have her portrait painted, a trip across Canada, a visit with Queen Mary in London, the opportunity to be part of the Miss America contest, and the chance to do a screen test for the movies.

The goodies did not come along as promised. She went to New York for the screen test, but decided not to go through with it at the last minute. Winifred's manager, Walter Golding, refused to allow her to get involved with the Miss America contest, as he thought it was too commercial. Winifred did some travelling within the Maritimes, though her trip to England never happened. She was actually the first woman to ever sit in the legislature in Fredericton, and the first

Postcard of Winifred Blair decked out for a skating competition at Lily Lake in 1923

woman to be allowed down into the mines at Glace Bay, Nova Scotia.

It was when she was on a trip to Moncton that Winifred became connected to Quispamsis. She was travelling in a private car usually used by the railway's top officials, and when the train reached Quispamsis, it was compelled to pull into a siding so a freight train could pass. According to local tradition, the area of the track where Winifred's car was stopped has since been known as the Blair Siding after the first Miss Canada.

After a flurry of attention throughout the summer of 1923, Winifred Blair's story was largely forgotten. Another Miss Canada competition wasn't held until 1946, and by then few people remembered the identity of the very first winner.

Sly as a fox

Clifford Shaw, who grew up in Grand Bay, recalls that in the early 1950s an iron foundry known as Thompson Manufacturing Company stood on the hill behind the current Irving Blue Canoe. The boys he grew up with took him deep into the woods to the west of the foundry and showed him the remnants of cages from a fox farm that had operated in the area. The road they travelled on to reach the cages was Fox Ranch Road. Though this name is no longer used for the road in Grand Bay, in Rothesay, Exit 133 off the Mackay Highway, leading down to Old Hampton Road is known as Fox Farm Road.

Fox farming was a big industry in New Brunswick, beginning with John H. Oulton's operations at Shemogue in 1910. It spread from there to Prince Edward Island and Nova Scotia. By the mid-1920s, the industry had reached its zenith—there were farms throughout the southern part of New Brunswick, in Salisbury and the lower Kennebecasis where Fox Farm Road runs today. There were at least four other fox farms in the Kennebecasis Valley within what is now the main business district of Quispamsis.

A bottomless lake and limestone hills

In 1920, when David H. Waterbury walked from central Saint John to Gondola Point he observed a number of features that can still be seen to this day. Waterbury's notes on the train tracks that cross Lawlor Lake and the crenated limestone in the Brookville Hills may prompt people to look at these familiar sites in a new light.

The European and North American Railway began in Saint John in 1853, and was destined to terminate in Shediac. According to Waterbury, it nearly terminated at ninety-metre (three-hundred-foot) wide Lawlor Lake. He wrote: "To state the length of time and cost of filling and effort to get a foundation for the track here, one would run the risk of being considered a prevaricator; the amount would be thought fabulous. The place began to be considered a bottomless pit or that it went through to the antipodes. A statement of possible credence is that it is part of the crater of an extinct volcano."

To this day, there are people who say the lake is bottomless.

Of the Brookville Hills overlooking the lake, Waterbury noted that the "dark old-looking excavation in the limestone hills" was the place that "stone used in the construction of the Cathedral" was taken nearly seventy years ago. Waterbury was referring to the Cathedral of the Immaculate Conception, a building he would have passed on Waterloo Street while on his journey. The initial stone for the cathedral was brought to the city in the early 1850s. Every massive piece needed to construct the building was moved by horse and wagon.

Sleeping Princess Hills

According to Native lore the hills that rise over the Kennebecasis River take the shape of a maiden reclining on her side, awaiting the return of her brave with food captured during a successful hunt. Another legend says that the hills form the outline of Glooscap, who laid down to rest before a battle with the Ossekeag Indians and never woke up, as the enemy put a sleeping potion in his drink. It is not hard to imagine either of these stories when gazing at the Sleeping Princess Hills of Long Island, the Kingston Peninsula, and Long Reach from the knoll of the Mackay Highway leading to the Gondola Point Arterial.

The river becomes the road

Passage from Saint John to Fredericton became much easier when the Kennebecasis and St. John rivers froze over. Winter travellers could use an ice road that began in Renforth and ran in a fairly straight line from the shore of the Kennebecasis to the Green in Fredericton. The road went from what was then called New Portage Cove to Moss Glen, across the Kingston Peninsula and up the river via the Long Reach, passing Oak Point, Evandale, Gagetown, and Burton, before running into the Queen City. If conditions were good, this trip would take between four and six hours. The trip from Saint John to Fredericton was an overnight journey during the summer, so it was quite a bonus when the winter conditions cooperated and thick ice was formed; however, all too often the ice was not thick enough all the way along the route, and lives were lost in the name of speed.

A night at the movies

On July 18, 1952, the Grand Bay Drive-in opened for business in Martinon. The feature movie on that night was *Tulsa* starring Susan Hayward, Robert Preston, and Pedro Armendariz. The second movie shown was a comedy with the Bowery Boys.

Before the opening, the drive-in's owners, J. M. Franklin, Mitchell Franklin, Peter Herschorn, and Samuel A. Babb, assured the public that every convenience would be on hand at the outdoor theatre. The owners promised that shows would change three times a week, and would be held rain or shine. Admission was sixty cents for adults and twenty-five cents for students, and children under twelve were free, so there was no

Newspaper ad for the first showing at the Grand Bay drive-in

need for a babysitter. Patrons were served in their cars by attendants. The theatre featured thirteen rows of speakers, and enough room for three hundred cars.

The drive-in proved popular with the public, and its success spawned a competitor—the Fundy Drive-In on Manawagonish Road, which operated from 1956 to 1964. The Highway Drive-In at Colton Brook Road off the Mackay Highway opened in 1966 using, it is believed, the equipment from the Fundy Drive-In in its less foggy location in the Kennebecasis Valley. Both the Highway and the Grand Bay drive-ins closed in 1983. Today, the nearest drive-in to Saint John is in Sussex.

Lost in translation

Don't expect to find only people of French descent living in French Village, the stretch of Route 860 ten kilometres (six miles) southwest of Hampton, today; however, that was certainly the case in 1767. The land was originally part of a grant of Pierre Chesnet, Sieur de Breuil. Sometime after 1769, ten families who likely paddled up the Hammond River began farming the area. They did so successfully until 1783, when they were displaced by the influx of Loyalist settlers that arrived following the American Revolution. Recently a graveyard discovered in the area has yielded some information about the original settlers, who are believed to have moved as far off as Madawaska County when they were displaced. In Hammond River Park, a boulder marked with the year 1714 and four squares is thought to have been engraved with some sort of message by these French settlers. Some believe the inscription denoted land ownership, while others think it would lead to treasure if they could intepret the message. Still others believe it to be a hoax.

A biblical message

Without a doubt, the most eye-catching feature of St. David's United Church on the Rothesay Common is the biblical quote that adorns the area over the pediments on the front of the church. The quote reads: "Man Does Not Live By Bread Alone."

Long-time church member George Robinson says the message was placed on the church to honour Reverend Bill Titus, who had once used the line in a sermon. Before Titus left the church, the letters of the words were cut out and used as a puzzle at a reception to honour the popular minister, who had served the church in the 1970s. Later, the church board of directors decided to permanently place the message over the pediments as a lasting tribute to Reverend Bill Titus.

Today the words are considered by many passersby who might not otherwise read one line of scripture. Once, however, the message became a bit confusing when the letter n fell off the first word, leaving the humorous message, "Ma Does Not Live By Bread Alone."

A royal odour

It could reasonably be assumed that Regal Drive received its name because a king or queen once visited the area in Quispamsis, but the true source of the street's name is quite surprising. The name is derived from Regal Skunk Works, which was once located on the road that connects Colonial Drive and Chamberlain Road. At the factory, a most unusual operation extracted the liquid from skunk glands to enhance perfume.

A banana split with a breathtaking view

In 1962, the Hamm farm in Grand Bay, which had a stunning view of the St. John River, was selected as the location of the area's first Dairy Queen. Emily McCoy began working there in 1970, and became part owner with Ellsworth Mitton in 1978. She recalls with fondness the visits of three provincial premiers. "Richard Hatfield loved our banana splits," she says with a chuckle. "Frank McKenna began his campaigns by taking a photo with the bay in the background, and later, Bernard Lord did the same thing. They bought ice cream, too," she says.

McCoy says the location provides "a million-dollar view," and it's a view that she believes is in photographs taken by visitors from all across the country, and from countries around the world. Since 2004, no ice cream has been sold at the spot, but the view of the widest portion of the St. John River, the Grand Bay, is still as charming as ever.

Memorial to a tragic race

Almost everyone living in Renforth is aware of the sculling race that took place on August 28, 1871, on the Kennebecasis River between Torryburn Cove and Kingshurst. A crowd of thousands from Saint John, and indeed, from across the nation, looked on as James Renforth, a British oarsman, died while trying to defeat the Paris Crew from Saint John. The death of the twenty-nine-year-old shocked the crowd. The

Harry (Bud) Nice in 1907. Sculling was a popular harbour sport in Saint John from the 1860s onwards

name of the area, which had been known as the Chalet, was changed to Renforth in his honour in October 1913.

Thousands of people were told the story as children, but until 1996, no permanent memorial to the incident existed. That year, an artisan named Madeline Hilton Moore created a model of the Paris Crew's boat, made using a template of the actual thirteen metre (forty-two foot) craft, which is in storage in the New Brunswick Museum. She mounted her six metre (nineteen foot) bronze boat on granite rocks, on which she carved sketches that symbolize life along the Kennebecasis. One of the most curious parts of the work is Moore's inclusion of sixteen variations of the spelling Kennebecasis.

A perilous journey

In the winter of 1848, travel between Saint John and Fredericton was offered by competing stagecoach lines that often took chances as they vied for customers. One service advertised that it left Saint John at 7:00 am three days a week, on Tuesdays, Thursdays, and Saturdays. The return from Fredericton left at 6:00 am on Mondays, Wednesdays, and Fridays. The trip took one full day, but only if conditions were favourable; if not, it could turn into a two- or three-day journey, with stops at one of the many stagecoach inns along the way.

From time to time, tragedies occurred during the trips, as the stagecoaches sometimes took shortcuts over the frozen river. One incident was described in the *New Brunswick Courier* on January 28, 1848:

On Tuesday evening last, as Mr. James Hewitt's stage, driven by his eldest son, was returning from Fredericton, it unfortunately went into an opening in the ice in Grand Bay and two of the passengers lost their lives. A third passenger, Mr. George Morrow of Oromocto and the driver were saved. The accident occurred a short distance from the shore and the cries of help were heard by Mr. McCorsky whose house was about half a mile distant. He hastened to the spot and afforded all assistance in his power. The two persons who perished were Mrs. Mary Taylor and a Mr. Gatley.

Neither the *Courier* nor the *Morning News* commented on the possibility of an investigation or inquest, nor did they note if the horses had perished. Both papers reported that the bodies had been recovered, and the *Morning News* added that the coach had been retrieved. The *Morning News* also added a comment that may seem strange today, but that may have been commonplace when such accidents happened regularly. The copy read: "We sincerely deplore Mr. Hewitt's loss. He and his son (who drives) have always been polite and obliging to travelers and others—and we hope he will do enough business during the remainder of the season to compensate him for his loss."

An imaginative
initiation ritual

How Millionaire's Hill, between Hampton Road and the Mackay Highway via Renshaw Road, got its name isn't exactly clear—whether it was named for its wealthy residents, or the grand million-dollar view from the pinnacle isn't know for certain.

Others call it by the more mundane name of Mackay Hill. Long-time Rothesay resident Tim Ellis prefers to call it Spy Glass Hill. Whatever it's called, the view that the hill provides makes it a great place for a jaunt. From the top you can see the town, with its church steeples and water tower punching up over the treeline, the shining waters of the far-off Kennebecasis River, Long Island, and the rock crevices known as the Minister's Face.

Ellis cautions that it is important to be on the watch for "snipes" on any venture to the area. He says that incoming residents of nearby Rothesay Collegiate School would be taken to the base of the hill at night, and made to crawl on their hands and knees to the top searching for "snipes." "Of course, there is no such thing," he laughed, as he shared his story of the famous private school's initiation ritual.

Magnificent mud

The town of Quispamsis announced in May 1984 that a nature trail would be built at Mud Lake. It was not the sort of place most people thought of as a natural area that they could enjoy—no beaches, not much in the way of trees, not a canoe-ing or kayak location, just a tiny lake surrounded by a soggy marsh that has been encroached on by the Hampton Highway and Gondola Point Arterial. The town's own maintenance staff had been using the edge of the marsh as a place to store salt and sand.

If Mud Lake was to retain its important roles as a habitat for marsh birds and a filter for rainwater that drained toward bet-ter-known Ritchie Lake, it needed attention. It wasn't an easy job, but Duncan Kelbaugh, the owner of Brunswick Nurseries who had undertaken the job for the Town of Quispamsis, found a way to build boardwalks and trails through the ten-hectare (twenty-five-acre) bog with minimum disturbance to the remaining marsh. His combination of spongy pathways and wooden walkways led to the shore of 0.8 hectare (two-acre) Mud Lake itself. Today, the area is a delight to visit year-round. One part of the trail that runs over a floating bog is not to be missed; it depresses underfoot, as it is truly dry land floating on the water table.

A dramatic entrance

At the entrance to Kennebecasis Park, four pillars let those driving through know that they have entered the sub-division. For three-quarters of a century, these pillars stood on Mecklenburg Street in Saint John's South End to let those passing through know that they were entering the grounds of Senator W. H. Thorne's home. His very ornate house stood on a rise behind the pillars, and a circular driveway led up to the house. From 1878 until about 1910, horse-drawn carriages would have passed by the gates. After the very early part of the twentieth century motor vehicles would have been the norm at Senator Thorne's, just as they are today at Kennebecasis Park.

Party at the Frog Pond

The riverboat era began on the St. John River in 1816 with the *General Smyth*. Riverboats are often associated with the St. John River, but riverboat travel was also a popular way to reach destinations along the Kennebecasis River between Saint John and Hampton, including Renforth, Rothesay, Quispamsis, and Gondola Point.

The era of riverboats slowly ended once train service became available in the valley in 1858, and north from Saint John in 1869. The *D. J. Purdy*, the last boat to serve the area, had a connection with both the St. John and Kennebecasis rivers, and

The riverboat **D.J. Purdy** *before it ended its days as a dance hall at Gondola Point.*

its final voyage was to Gondola Point. There it was beached in an area known as the Frog Pond. As the riverboat's owner, Jack Jones, filled its hull with sand, he had visions of turning it into a dance hall, with a casino and slot machines. He also had liquor available. None of this was legal at the time, and even if it had been, it certainly did not fit in with the bucolic nature of the Gondola Point Beach area. Some believe a mysterious fire that ripped through the area in 1948, destroying the *D. J. Purdy*, was set by someone who wanted the old boat out of the area, while others think it was burnt to collect the insurance to pay back taxes. Whatever happened, the fire brought a 130-year riverboat era to a flaming end.

House of gold

There are many fine homes in the Kennebecasis Valley, but few look as if they were plucked from the English countryside and dropped in the area. Dunanore Castle on Route 100 in Brookville was built in 1914 for Peter Drake, overseas buyer for Manchester Robertson Allison, the grand department store. He may have seen a similar house while on a buying trip in England. The castle with the Celtic name that means "house of gold" was built by R. C. Donald of Moncton. It features exterior stone quarried from the Brookville Hills, and the interior contains beamed and panelled rooms, and a sunroom and games room, which weren't found in many houses built in 1914.

The Drakes lived there until 1947, when they sold the house to the Nodells for six thousand dollars, which seems a low figure considering its grandeur. The family added extensive gardens to the property. Upon Nodell's death in 1962, the house sat empty for the first time in fifty years. In 1964, the family that bought the house had children, and for the first time youngsters lived on the property. Real estate agent Kevin Butler's behind the scenes look at many Kennebecasis area properties in the *Telegraph Journal* was the source of this information about Dunanore.

The view from the top

There are at least five mountains in New Brunswick that are known as Bald Mountain. The name was chosen because each has a bare, rocky peak that protrudes above the treeline.

In 1936, Walter H. Golding, manager of the Capitol (Imperial) Theatre and regular contributor of arts-related material to the *Evening Times Globe*, took a day off and travelled to the Browns Flat area, where he climbed the peak that he had long known as Bald Mountain (though he told readers that its name had been changed to Mount Champlain). In a complete account of his adventure, he described an arduous walk to the top of the mountain, 457 metres (1,500 feet) above sea level. At the end of his climb he was greeted by Signalman Crozier, whose job was to watch for fires from the peak. As a result of his work, Crozier, described as an "amiable host," was adept at pointing out the lakes, rivers, and other mountains that can be seen in the 105-kilometre (65-mile) radius viewable from atop Mount Champlain. Golding spotted the Admiral Beatty Hotel, which stood next to the Capitol (Imperial) Theatre that he managed. Golding was surprised, upon signing the guest book, to learn that 487 people had made the climb to the top in 1935.

Prince's Beach
"fit for the gods"

The portion of the St. John river between Westfield's Brundage Point and Harding's Point on the Kingston Peninsula is easily crossed by ferry today, but this wasn't always the case. In 1907, a plan to develop the area around Harding's Point may have failed because it was not as accessible as it now is. Rather than Harding's Point, the area was called Prince's Beach by the proponents of the development, aptly known as the Prince's Beach Company. On the beach stood a tree that was renamed the Prince of Wales elm after the prince admired it when he travelled up the river in August 1860. The company that planned to develop a three-kilometre (two-mile) stretch along the river, located between Prince's Beach and Sand Point, described the landscape as "fit for the gods."

To promote the idea of development in the area, the company held a limerick contest that included prizes of cottage lots in the area. As a publicity aid, the company purchased a painting of the Prince of Wales elm that they hoped to present to the reigning monarch, Edward VII. Contest entrants were given halftones of the same image, which would become a valued copy of the painting if the king accepted the gift. The value of each cottage lot was between $50 and $100, and the principal lot, which included the Clark house, was valued at $2,500. The proposed development was never constructed, but there may still be some of those halftones of the famous tree in cottages or homes in the area.

Country camp for city kids

One of the Gyro Club of Saint John's most visible projects was its Fresh Air Camp, located on a bluff between former Highway 102 and the St. John River at Grand Bay. The camp opened in 1927, and during its existence, thousands of boys and girls went there to experience their first country holidays. The location of the camp is where the heart of Grand Bay's commercial district lies today. Swimming, cooking over an open fire, hiking, crafts, organized games, and lots of good food were hallmarks of the successful outings for city children who would otherwise not have had a holiday. The camp ceased operation in the early 1960s, and the club itself is no longer active. *More Up Country Memories* by Diane Bormke and Linda Aiton lists its years of operation as 1927 to 1964. The camp is now just a wonderful memory for the thousands who visited.

Model Farm leaves its mark

Stock Farm Road got its name when the Otty family rented land overlooking the Hammond River to the provincial government for use as a model farm in the 1880s. The farm was used to teach area farmers better methods for carrying out their work, and it proved a great success. Farmers came from miles around for training. Some came more often than they needed to, for they were treated well at the government operation, right down to a few good strong drinks to make their day all the more pleasurable.

Stock Farm as it appeared in 1999

Of course, this all cost money, and the farm ran a deficit. The legislature regularly debated the wisdom of continuing to run such an operation. Every member seemed sure that if the Model Farm were moved to their riding it would be run much more efficiently and within budget. Due to the farm's proximity to the Intercolonial Railway, the operation managed to endure long enough to ensure two roadways—Stock Farm and Model Farm roads—in the area took their name from its presence.

A forbidding land

Scotsman Peter Campbell's book, *Travels In the Interior Inhabited Parts of North America in the Years 1791 and 1792*, was the Frommer's Guide of its day. A century ago, W. O. Raymond was granted permission to transcribe the New Brunswick section of Campbell's book. Raymond said that the number of known copies of the rare book in America could "be counted on the fingers of one hand."

Campbell's narrative says he left Fort William in Scotland on June 11, 1791, and sailed to Saint John in fifty-six days. He gives observations of what he saw in the area just eight years after the Loyalist influx. Before visiting the Kennebecasis Valley, several people had told him "that it was among the best parts of the province, and fittest for new settlers, the easiest land to clear, and for raising stock the least trouble."

When Campbell actually visited the valley, accompanied by a Saint John merchant named Thomson, his faithful servant, and his dog, he was disappointed. He described the land as "uneven, knolly, barren and interspersed with many small lakes." He did note that the "abundance of trout" in the lakes was a redeeming feature of the area. The land was described as "timbered with pine and spruce," and Campbell noted that several people who had settled in the area had begun to clear the "poor and forbidding soil." His most damning comment was that the area "had nothing to recommend it but its vicinity to the city of Saint John."

One must not be too hard on Campbell for his assessment, for even as late at the early 1960s, experts did not predict the suburban development that has occurred in the valley.

General John Coffin of Nerepis

John Coffin began his military career at the Battle of Bunker Hill in Boston, and by the end of the Revolutionary War, he had risen to the rank of major. He came to New Brunswick with the Loyalists, and bought 2,428 hectares (6,000 acres) of land at the mouth of the Nerepis River, on which he built Alwington Manor. In 1786 he was elected to represent Kings County at the first sitting of the province's legislature, which was then held at Mallard House on King Street in Saint John where Brunswick Square stands today. His wife was the daughter of South Carolina's governor, and the couple had two sons and two daughters. As was customary at the time, the Coffin family had two black slaves, William Watson and Samuel Sleeves, and a female servant.

When Coffin was called back to England, he sold his estate to William Belyea who renamed it Woodman's Point. After completing his service overseas, Coffin returned to the Nerepis, but his wife did not. He brought with him fourteen boys from England, one of whom was William Blagdon. Coffin cleared land in the area of Sagwa, built houses, and spent time canoeing, hunting, and fishing. He was known for being generous to the poor, and he secured land for the Anglican Church to build on. He died at age eighty-seven, and is buried at the Church of England Cemetery at Woodman's Point. Beside his grave is a huge oak tree planted by William Blagdon in his memory.

Quispamsis's link to the past—Stoneycroft

Located at the highest point of Route 100, the main business route through Quispamsis, Stoneycroft is the town's best-known heritage structure. In the 1830s, an advertisement in the *New Brunswick Courier* described Stoneycroft (though it was not then known by that name) as "two hundred and fifty acres of good land, well situated, being 11 miles from St John, and on the post road leading to Halifax, with two good dwelling house (two stories high) and two good barns." It also said that the home was "well adapted for entertainment."

Researchers Vivian Wright and Nancy Fisher spend a lot of time trying to piece together the story of Stoneycroft. They discovered its first owner was Caleb Wetmore, who sold the building to John Stuart. Stuart then operated the property as an inn or a tavern, known as Wetmore's. Robert Keltie, a Saint John brewer, was the next owner, though he seems to have leased it out to Stuart, John Campbell, and John Wright. It was known as the Lakefield Inn for part of this time and also went under the name of Eleven Mile House, as it was a stagecoach stop. The name Stoneycroft was first used when David Magee and Matthew Manks bought the property in 1870. The name came from Magee's family home in Coleraine, Ireland.

In 1979, the house was designated a National Historic Site. Further research in the early 1980s by Wendy Field and Paula White confirmed the names of David Magee and Matthew Manks, and added the names of Andrew Thompson, William Kennedy, John Morris, the Robinson Family, and Jay and Stephen Delaney to the ownership list.

Bishop's picnic the highlight of the year

Torryburn refers to a cluster of homes located on or near Highway 100 between Drury Cove Road and Kennebecasis Park. The name is believed to come from Torryburn House, which appeared on an 1851 map, and may have been chosen by the owner as a remembrance of his birthplace in Scotland. A century ago, Torryburn was the site of a racetrack, located where Kennebecasis Park is today; a military grounds, in approximately the same location; and the Bishop's Picnic Grounds, in the woods and fields that now surround the Villa Madonna Retreat House.

Of the three, the picnic grounds were the best known. The Bishop's picnics were considered the highlight of the year for Catholic children. A 1925 report said that the picnics had been held for "more than threescore years," which means that

Saint John Rifle Company at Drury Cove Rifle Range, Torryburn, circa 1890

they began in 1855, when the Cathedral of the Immaculate Conception on Waterloo Street was finished.

In 1925, as always, children of the cathedral held a parade, which stretched from Oak Hall on upper King Street to Market Square in downtown Saint John. That year an estimated seven hundred children worked their way to Union Station, where a special train of twelve cars was waiting to take them to the Torryburn grounds at ten o'clock in the morning. As in years past, they were accompanied through the streets by the City Cornet Band and bandmaster James Connolly, who had led the band for fifty-one years. At the picnic grounds, they enjoyed the usual games, races, sport booths, fish pond, and of course, ice cream and liquid refreshments.

No place like home

Nowhere in the Saint John area are there as many homes with intriguing names as in the town of Rothesay. As the area developed slowly after the arrival of the railway in 1858, street numbering was not necessary, as everyone knew just about everyone else in the community. Many people with roots in England, Ireland, Wales, and Scotland followed the custom of naming, rather than numbering their houses, as was the tradition in their home countries. Robert Hook and Ann Condon's book, *Rothesay: An Illustrated History 1784–1920,* is full of details about the area's homes and their names including: The Willows, Balmaghie, The Birdcage, Shadow Lawn, Blantyre, Ballantyne House, Ravenswood, White Spruces, The Knoll, Deerpath Farm, the Purds, Strathnaver, Kingshurst, Netherwood, Karsalie, Bircholme, Whitling Cottage, and Firshade.

Flagpoles and wormholes

When the Prince of Wales visited Saint John in 1860, he was taken to Rothesay in order to catch the riverboat *Forest Queen* to Fredericton. The boat was tied up at a wharf that Honourable John Robertson had built. Robertson thought there should be a flagpole flying the Union Jack on the wharf, so he had it erected. If the prince noted the flagpole, it is not mentioned in accounts of the departure. It was, however, noticed by a member of the Robertson family, who used it for target practice for years following the royal visit. A story in the January 1898 issue of the magazine *Gripsack* reported that the flagstaff "finally became so honeycombed by rifle bullets that it tumbled to the ground." Robertson had no explanation for the destruction of the flagpole until the family marksman told him that it had probably "become worm eaten." The report concludes by saying that the "explanation from the 'practical joker' was satisfactory" to Mr. Robertson.

Skirts for safekeeping

One story of hardship and cunning with a Kennebecasis Valley connection is that of Loyalist Charity Newton, which was contributed to *New Brunswick Magazine* by W. O. Raymond. She was forced to come to Canada after the Revolutionary War, as her husband, Ebenezer, incurred ill will from his American neighbours because he had served on the side of the British.

By the early years of the nineteenth century, she was determined to go home to Rhode Island for a visit. She took her baby, a basket of food, and a barrel of produce from the garden to show her parents she was not living in hunger in New Brunswick, which was thought of as unproductive and barren land by Americans. After arriving at home she was warmly welcomed by her very old mother, who thought Charity looked coarse and tired as a result of the toil and hard life of twenty-five years as a pioneer in New Brunswick.

After a lengthy visit, Charity embarked on a ship out of New York. It soon became clear that the ship was going to be overtaken by a French ship whose aim was to plunder and sink Charity's vessel. The captain of Charity's ship had a stock of silver dollars he wished to save, and he asked if she would help by quilting them between her petticoats. When the boat was taken by the French, the captain, with characteristic politeness, declined to "molest madame" and the coins remained undiscovered. Charity Newton returned to the Kennebecasis Valley with a great story to share. Whether or not she was able to hang onto any of those silver coins to make her life a little more comfortable is unknown.

The price of faith

The waiting room of the station house at Rothesay, which still stands today, was the scene of the first Sunday afternoon service for what was to become St. David's Church. This service was conducted by Reverend William MacDonald, who was minister of St. Andrew's Presbyterian Church in Saint John. Rothesay was known then as Scribner's Corner.

During the summer of 1859 a small group met and decided to build a Presbyterian church. Land was offered by Honourable John Robertson for this purpose. Robert Thomson Sr. was appointed secretary-treasurer to the committee, and collected most of the funds necessary to finish the building. The Rothesay Presbyterian Church was formally opened on Friday, August 17, 1860.

At the request of the residents, and by courtesy of the presbytery, occasional Episcopal services were held in the church beginning in the spring of 1861. The privilege was continued until 1867.

For the Presbyterians, the construction cost of seven hundred pounds was a very serious financial burden, and by the mid-1870s the congregation was unable to meet the mortgage and it was foreclosed by a court order. The church was sold at public auction at Chubb's Corner in Saint John for $1,200. Ironically, it was purchased by the Episcopalians, who had been allowed to use the church at no charge. The building was renamed St. Paul's Anglican Church, and is still in use to this day.

The early Presbyterians gradually recovered from the loss of their church, and about 1886 they arranged to use the Rothesay Methodist Church for their services. On August 2, 1887, the Presbyterians decided that although a church was beyond their means, they would build a church hall, and in 1888 the original frame for what was to become St. David's Church on the Common was built by E. J. Rodd for $1,200. Thus, there were once again two Protestant churches fronting on the Common and to this day, both are doing well.

West of the River

When the Loyalists arrived in Saint John in 1783, some received lots on the west side of the harbour; among them was the city's first mayor, Gabriel G. Ludlow. It soon became clear that the east side would be the business heart of the city, and from the beginning west siders had to cross the open water of the harbour to do business with government. It was not an easy process, because until 1853 a ferry was the only way to get to town. Thus, west siders developed their own independent community, based initially on shipbuilding and milling of timber, and after 1900, on the presence of the Canadian Pacific Railway, which had chosen the west side docks as its eastern terminus for the winter season. West siders proudly said they did not need to travel to town for anything during this period, though from 1835 until it was finally completed in 1968, they never stopped agitating for a bridge that would allow them to travel to where they said they did not need to go. This section explores the life of this area through its buildings, people, and day-to-day events, showing the independent spirit of this part of the city.

Baker's Castle

Designed by F. Neil Brodie, and built of limestone from the Randolph and Baker Mills at Greenhead, this 1915 castle stands on the Westfield Road overlooking South Bay. Baker's Castle was owned by Parker Baker's family as a private residence. It originally cost twenty-five thousand dollars to build. The stonework was completed by MacDonald of Sussex, and the woodwork by J. Medley Belyea, a West Side firm. It is often called Emerson's Castle, as Senator Clarence V. Emerson bought the building after it had been used as an inn for several years. Today it is owned by the Craft family.

Baker's Castle in South Bay in 1981.

Kettles, and clocks, and pie…oh my!

On June 9 and 10, 1965, Kmart Canada held a job fair to attract staff for the planned opening of the national chain's first location in New Brunswick at the Lancaster Mall on Fairville Boulevard. Of the ten Kmart stores in Canada, the Saint John store was to be the largest at eighty thousand square feet. For many years after it was built, the store was one of the chain's top producing locations.

The Kmart opening on August 5, 1965, created at least two hundred new jobs for west siders. Store management also promised to buy 90 percent of the Saint John Kmart's goods in Canada, so the trickle effect was considerable. Opening day prices included: sets of six coffee mugs for ninety-seven cents; alarm clocks for one dollar and ninety-nine cents; and toothpaste for thirty-seven cents. Turkey dinner was served in the cafeteria for sixty-nine cents, while a slice of cherry pie cost only twenty cents. W. Neil Kennedy, a native of Saint John, was the first manager of the city's Kmart. He had risen up through the ranks of S. S. Kresge, Kmart's founders, and returned home to manage the new store. It closed in 1996.

A tragic turn

On the former King's Highway—the main route from Saint John to Fredericton—now called the Westfield Road, a very sharp left turn just beyond the Acamac Backland Road and just before Byroad 7 has been the scene of many serious accidents over the years. Locally it is known as Suicide Corner. Though no changes have been made to the turn in recent times, it is thankfully no longer the scene of as many tragic traffic accidents as it was fifty years ago.

A memorable memorial

Astone erected on the Lorneville Road in August 2004 says the site was the location of the Pisarinco Anglican Church, a daughter church of St. Anne's in Musquash, from 1860 to 1900. The ubiquitous epitaph of one Sam Dean is found in this graveyard. It reads:

Remember me as you pass by,
    As you are now, so once was I,
    As I am now,
    So you must be,
    Prepare yourself to follow me.

One itinerant minister added:
    To follow you I'm not content
    Until I find out, which way you went.

Zanzibar Restaurant

Located at 204 King Street West, the original home of the well-known clothing establishment, the Ideal Stores, the Zanzibar was *the* meeting place for west siders seeking mates from 1958 to 1960, when it was operated by Leslie E. Agate. Its phone number was OX4-9184, and Agate seems to have lived on-site, likely in an apartment upstairs. This must have been a challenge, as the Zanzibar was not known as a quiet place. Some west siders can only recall that it was a place they were warned to avoid—the Zanzibar had a bit of an unsavoury reputation due to its popularity with a wilder crowd.

Avery's Corner

We call it Simm's Corner today, when we are being polite—but we call it Haywire Corner when trying to navigate the triangle with no traffic lights that separates traffic coming south from Main Street, going north on Lancaster Avenue, travelling east from Raynes Avenue, and heading west from Bridge Road.

In 1834, the spot was known as Avery's Corner, as Richard Avery operated a pleasure grounds on the embankment overlooking the Reversing Falls. Avery promised that the wonderful view of the surrounding countryside from Hamilton's Hill would "repay the visitor for the trouble of the walk." He had a tea garden, but also sold "wines and liquor of the first quality" for those looking for a more bracing libation. You could visit for the day, or stay for longer in Avery's cottages. This was a

This 1950s tourist bureau marks where Hamilton Hill would have been

long time ago, before the first bridge was built in 1853, so to reach Avery's property one had to take a ferry from town, and then make the half-hour walk from Rodney Slip to the heights of Lancaster. Hamilton's Hill became the site of the Provincial Hospital in 1848. J. D. Irving has owned the property since 1996, and it is now called Wolastoq Park.

Tough climb for a jellyfish

Fossils of jellyfish that swam in the ocean 550 million years ago have been found in the rocks of Courtenay Hill, according to geologist Randy Miller of the New Brunswick Museum. The hill, which is bounded by Watson, Duke, Olive and Prince streets, is one of only three places in the world (Poland and Alberta are the others) where jellyfish fossils of that age have been discovered. Geologists believe that the hill was once part of the continent of Africa.

Limey Land

In the early 1960s an influx of men from England began teaching in the Saint John school system. Among them was Roger Woolway, who was assigned to New Albert School. He began to use the filled-in millpond area between Rodney and St. John streets as a soccer field. His team was soon playing other schools that also had coaches who were English immigrants. The field was soon known as Limey Land, nicknamed for the sound of the teachers barking orders in the distinctive cockney accent. Up to that date, the field did not have an official name. Since then, a ball field has been built at the southern portion, a pumping station in the middle, and tennis courts and a playground on the north end, and it's officially known as the Carleton Ball Diamond. Roger Woolway died in January 2005.

A symbolic salmon

The placement of a wooden fish over the door of Lorneville's Presbyterian Church in 1885 by W. C. Caulder, the church's first minister, was cause for controversy. One of Lorneville's oldest residents, W. T. Galbraith, shared this information with the *Evening Times Globe* in 1946, though he didn't say why the fish was controversial. The salmon was carved by an unnamed Saint John workman and was placed under a sign that read "Pisarinco." Pisarinco, meaning "ring-like cove," was the native name for the village prior to 1902, when the name Lorneville was adopted after the Marquis of Lorne visited Saint John. The fish not only represents Lorneville industry (as many as sixty salmon boats once worked out of the village), but also the fact that several of Christ's Apostles were fishermen. The fish was an ancient symbol that Christians used to secretly identify one another.

The salmon over the door of the Lorneville United (Presbyterian) Church was controversial in 1885

Occupations and revolutions

The story of Lady La Tour's defence of Fort La Tour during the seventeenth century is familiar to nearly everyone. Another fort, which was located on the west side of Saint John Harbour, has an equally interesting history that dates back to the days of La Tour and his archrival Charnisay. Fort Manacoche was located on a little hill opposite Navy Island at the foot of King Street. It was first occupied by La Tour's son-in-law, Martin d'Aprendestiguy, Sieur de Martignon.

When Fort Louisbourg was surrendered to the British, General Moncton led an expedition to occupy Fort Manacoche. English settlement began in Saint John when the forty British soldiers landed near the old fort. They renamed it Fort Frederick, and for a month six hundred men were employed in restoring it, for it had fallen into decay after the French occupation. The fort was garrisoned until 1768, when troops were withdrawn because of unrest in New England over the Stamp Act, one of the events that led up to the American Revolution.

Fort Frederick remained under civil administration for several years until, in the first hostile act of the American Revolution, a party of rebels from Machias, Maine, entered Saint John Harbour in a sloop and burned the fort. They also captured a brig of 120 tons carrying oxen, sheep, and swine intended for the British troops in Boston. Old Fort Frederick holds a unique place in history as it spans the days from the French regime to the American Revolution.

Dutiful drinkers

In 1823 John I. Venner began selling gin at four pounds, six shillings per gallon. The gin was being distilled in Carleton for the first time, and was intended to fill demand that up to that time had been met only through European imports—or through smuggled goods. The product was said to be equal in quality to "Ane Hollands," but priced much lower. The public was invited to "examine for themselves" the local gin. No doubt many west siders considered it their patriotic duty to do so!

Inspiration in the Fundy fog

Poet Bliss Carman spent at least part of two summers, and perhaps more time, in West Saint John between 1882 and 1884. The book *Quest and Revolt* by Murial Miller, refers to letters Carman wrote to his parents and visits he made when they were at Mrs. Scampers guest house on the coast of the Bay of Fundy. Just where this house was remains a mystery, but perhaps on a foggy day he was inspired to write one of his poems that reflects on Saint John. These include "The Ships of Saint John," which includes the line: "Swing You Tides up out of Fundy, Blow You White Fog in from Sea."

...and the streets were paved with gold!

On January 14, 1863, a writer using the pen name Knickerbocker Jr. wrote to the *Daily News* and predicted that Courtenay Hill would one day feature an elegant street called Carleton Terrace, five kilometres (three miles) long and sixty metres (two hundred feet) wide with marble sidewalks. He said that Government House would be located on five tree-shaded acres (two hectares) of property along the street, and that a massive Gothic cathedral with eight bells, beautiful stained glass windows, and a magnificent organ would be close by. He described a pyramid-shaped public observatory containing expensive astronomical instruments. Finally, he wrote that a theatre and opera house would vie with each other for magnitude and grandeur. Today, we're lucky if the city keeps flags flying on Courtenay Hill's highest point.

The I. O. O. F. Hall

The Independent Order of Odd Fellows (I. O. O. F.) originated in eighteenth-century England, and King George IV was an early member. The organization's aim is to better the human race through educational and fraternal activity, and it grew rapidly in the days before governments began providing programs with similar goals. The I. O. O. F. became established in the United States in 1819 and in Canada in 1843. There were at least five I. O. O. F. lodges in Saint John when the Golden Rule Lodge began meeting in the Cornfield Hall on King Street. This led to the procurement of two lots on the corner of Guilford and Market Place, where the Greek-style hall that is now known as the I. O. O. F. Peerless Lodge No. 19 was built in 1893.

The hall is also the meeting place for the I. O. O. F.'s sister organizations, the Rebekah No. 37, the Sapphire, and the Jewel No. 6. The groups continue to carry out their benevolent work under the motto of "friendship, love, and truth." Though the organization now has fewer members than it once did, it continues to play an important role in the social and fraternal life of Saint John West.

Fiery conviction

According to Dr. Arthur Long, when the Carleton Public Hall burnt down on October 14, 1925, the Davis sisters, who had begun holding Pentecostal meetings at the hall, and had been asked to leave due to the noise, were quick to say publicly that the fire was retribution for their eviction. The sisters suffered through two more fires—one at the Magee Building and another at Venetian Gardens in the Berryman Building on February 5, 1933. After the Venetian Gardens fire, Carro Davis commented that it was the "third disaster of the kind to interfere with their work." They persevered, and by 1957 they

Saint John's impressive Imperial Theatre changed hands from being the Capitol Theatre to being the home of a Pentecostal congregation from 1957 to 1987

had developed such a following that they were able to buy the 1,500-seat Imperial Theatre (then known as the Capitol) for their church services. In 1987, they sold the building to the volunteer group that refurbished it into the magnificent Imperial Theatre, said by many visiting artists and companies to be the finest performance space in all of Canada.

NBTel dials the right number

Of the few brick-and-concrete buildings in Saint John West, thus one that catches people's eyes, is the NBTel Exchange Building at 244 Duke Street. Constructed in 1920, the building served the West Side as a switching station known as the Oxford Exchange. Growth in the number of NBTel customers created the need for an addition to the building in 1937. The addition, designed by architect H. Claire Mott, provided space for cable, a power plant, and a garage. On the ground floor one large room with no pillars accommodated the dial central office equipment, which became redundant with the advent of computers. NBTel promised to use, as far as possible, materials of New Brunswick manufacture to construct the building, rather than allowing the cost of materials to be the main consideration. Though no longer used by the telephone company, the original NBTel building is still standing and in use by a local business.

The glue of the community

The current Ketepec-Belmont-Morna (KBM) clubhouse on the corner of the Westfield Road and Acamac Beach Road is the second building to serve area residents' recreational needs since 1926. Photos on the clubhouse walls combine with the memories of older members, like Ben Rousell and Blair Perrin, to tell the story of how baseball, swimming, canoeing, dancing, tennis competitions, card parties, suppers, and playground activity have helped hold the community together over the years. Now, with third-generation participants coming through the door, the KBM is an example of how a community's can-do attitude and volunteer fundraising can produce great results in areas where the government does not provide adequate services.

Modern school's slow closure

When La Tour School opened on St. John Street in 1902, it was described as "thoroughly up to date in every respect," and "perhaps the finest in the city." The school, designed by H. H. Mott, had six classrooms and an exhibition hall or auditorium. It was designed to house 222 Protestant students who lived east of City Line and south of Rodney Street. The first principal was George E. Armstrong.

By 1956 the school was considered obsolete, and it closed—gradually. First, students in grades three to six started attending New Albert School, then a couple of years later, the rest of the students began to make the long walk to the school. The La Tour School was last used by the Cerebral Palsy Foundation, and thirty-three children were still utilizing the school in 1970, when it was condemned by the fire marshal. Soon after, the building was torn down. The site has apartments built on it today.

Braving the storm at Beacon Light

Beacon Light was a harbour navigation aid built atop a shoal off Beatteay's Beach (the Blue Rocks) in 1828. Along with the light on Partridge Island, the Beacon Light guided mariners safely into Saint John Harbour until it burned on January 7, 1867. It was rebuilt immediately. One of the most famous inci-

Postcard of the Beacon Light

dents at the Beacon Light took place during the Saxby Gale on the night of October 4, 1869. Lightkeeper James Earle thought it best to leave the Beacon during the storm—but once he experienced the swells, thought it safer to return. He did, and endured a horrible night as the water rose 2.5 metres (8 feet) higher than normal, but Earle lived to tell the tale. The Beacon Light came to an end when it was intentionally burned down on August 20, 1913, to get it out of the way so a safer channel could be made into the West Side docks.

World-famous fern fossils

Sedimentary rocks that are swept by Fundy tides on the shoreline between Seaside Park and Duck Cove became world famous between 1861 and 1863, when local geologist C. Fred Hartt brought them to the public's attention. He found fossils of Devonian-era plants in the grey sandstone and shale at the site. The rocks were easily chipped apart, not only by geologists from around the world, but by any west siders who made their way down the steep hill to the shore with a hammer and chisel. At the time, the property was owned by N. S. Demille and Zebedde Ring. The former's name is perpetuated in the name Demille Street, the closest street to the embankment where the fossils were, and are occasionally still found. The Ring Family still lives in the area, too.

No palm trees on this island

McCormack's Island cannot be found in either the bay or the river, or in any lake in Saint John West—this island was located at the intersection of Main Street, Manawagonish Road, and Church Avenue in the days before stoplights. Constable Charles McCormack of the Fairville Police Force would stand on the raised cement triangle directing traffic, and it soon carried his name. Constable McCormack, born in Milford, was a Lancaster police officer for over thirty years. He retired on July 1, 1965. According to Ron Humphrey, a Saint John police officer for thirty-one years, McCormack was known as a "super person to work with." He died in 1969.

A blaze at the mill

Built in 1899 at the head of Rodney Wharf, the La Tour Grain Mill, which employed twenty men, had the capacity to process 3,400 bushels of grain in twenty-four hours. The mill burned on the morning of July 12, 1914. At the time, it contained 6,000 bushels of corn, 2,500 bushels of oats, 1,000 bushels of wheat, 2,000 bushels of barley, and 7,000 bags of feed and meal. It was one of the last times that horses were used to pull the firefighting apparatus to the scene of a fire. The fire was blamed on an electrical fault, though others said that a cigarette or cigar dropped by a careless smoker had caused the blaze. The plant was covered by thirty-one thousand dollars in insurance. At the time of the fire, A. L. Fowler was the owner of the mill, and W. H. Fowler was its manager.

A prescription for beef and wine

On August 30, 1882, the *Daily Sun* reported that W. C. Rudman Allan had a thriving apothecary on lower King Street West. His most famed patent medicine was a beef, wine, and iron mixture. Its preparation must have taken much care and concentration, for painted on a walnut display case that was made for Allan by A. J. Charlton of Prince Street were the words, "Please don't converse with the dispenser."

A tongue twister for tourists

Tourists looking for accommodation in Saint John West are usually trying to find Ma...Ma...Mana...Manawag... Manawagonish Road, which rolls easily off natives' tongues, but is a mouthful for visitors. The Mi'kmaq word meaning "place of clams" refers to clam flats at Saint Rest's beach, which can be seen from the heights of Manawagonish Road. Both the heights and the marsh are products of the ice age, and Manawagonish Road is at the top of a glacial deposit of gravel. The Manawagonish Marsh is said to have been the original mouth of the St. John River, before the ice-age deposits of gravel blocked the river off, and it began to flow, as it does today, into the harbour via the Reversing Falls.

Bum the dog makes news in Boston

Roy Dryden of Moncton inherited a scrapbook that contained the story of his grandfather, grocer Archie Dryden, and his smart dog, Bum. Bum left Archie's Queen Street store each November to spend the winter guarding the busy freight-holding sheds of Saint John West. He would not return home until the Canadian Pacific Railway workers packed up their equipment and headed to Montreal in the spring. This went on for seventeen years—and the story of the smart dog was carried in 1939 by the *Saint John Evening Times Globe*, the *Montreal Star*, and the *Boston Globe*. Only at Christmas would Bum return to Queen Street to visit his owner for a few hours.

The place to shop

Emerson's Hardware, located on the corner of King and Ludlow streets from December 8, 1930, until fire wiped it out in November 26, 1957, was *the* place for west siders to shop. The Emersons were considered leading entrepreneurs in Saint John West. When it opened, the hardware store was described as a green-painted building, with the name Emerson spelled out in gold letters over well-lit display windows. The interior was lit by eight large electric lamps, and was tastefully decorated in oak. The description noted that the building gave the head of King Street, West Saint John's business centre, an imposing appearance. The

Emerson family's success was visible in the details of the homes they built, such as the stained glass window in William E.'s house at 139 Ludlow Street, which can be seen to this day. The store on King Street became West Saint John's first liquor store in 1958, and is now a convenience store.

Peck's special condiment

Peckham Joyce is remembered as one of the characters who made the West Side an interesting place to live. Joyce's first business was a grocery store on St. George Street, which opened in 1941. In 1942 it was known as Joyce's Ice Cream Parlour. By 1945 Peckham Joyce's Ice Cream Parlour was located at 175 Market Place. Peckham Joyce was famous for his ash-covered hot dogs. He almost always had a cigarette in his mouth—and when he made a hot dog, cigarette ashes went on the dog along with mustard and relish. The ice cream parlour closed in 1969.

The Flats

Today, when the Flats are spoken of, it is generally with reference to the mud flats of Beatteay's Beach, or the sand flats off Bay Shore Beach or McLaren's Beach. In the past, Beaconsfield Heights and the Lancaster Vale (the area around Bleury Street between Sand Cove Road and Fairville Boulevard) were sometimes called the Flats, instead of the Vale. In the 1880s a group of Irish settlers lived in a cluster of makeshift cottages behind Main Street in Fairville known as Paddy's Flats. This area between the rail line and the river was a convenient place for new immigrants who worked in nearby industries like the Cushing Mill, Ready Breweries, the clay and brick works, and the rail yards, to live.

Whirlpools at the falls

Fishermen called the largest whirlpool in the Reversing Falls "the pot." It forms between the Split Rock and the west shore of the gorge as the tide drops in the harbour, and is especially powerful in the spring. Champlain noted it in his narratives, and said the Natives would shoot arrows with pelts attached to them into the pot in hopes of impaling them on a great log caught in the whirlpool. The Natives believed that

"The pot" is at the right end of the rapids

this would appease the gods that lay in the depths of the water, who were showing their anger by creating the whirlpool.

The whirlpool known as the pot may have also been called Rankine's Eddy. The second name is mentioned in a July 14, 1894, report that describes how Edward and Daniel Logan and John McBay had left Indiantown on Thursday night to go "pot hunting—gathering debris, logs, etc." Their boat was found "bottom up in Rankine's Eddy" at five-thirty the next morning. Although shouts were heard at Cushing's Mill at one in the morning, no action was taken. Later, it was discovered the accident was caused by broken thole-pins on the gunwale, which are the oarlocks of the vessel.

Hunch Rock

Jack Sweet shared the story behind the unusually named Hunch Rock near Prospect Point in the Reversing Falls. A boat out in Marble Cove was caught in the tide change, and sucked into the rapids between Goat Island and Prospect Point. The woman in the boat managed to throw her child to safety on the point, and the rock took the family's name, Hunch, after the incident.

Marching to a different beat

The first band to cross the present Reversing Falls Bridge was the City Cornet Band on July 1, 1915. The band had been at Seaside Park for the day, and while the bridge was not officially open, it was crossable. Though the band had planned to cross the 1853 suspension bridge to return to the city, when it was suggested they "make a record" by becoming the first to cross the new bridge, they could not resist following bandmaster Frank Waddington and tootling their way from west to east.

The cut-off point

The first link of the improved Highway 7 between Saint John West and Fredericton began at Carvell's Farm where Manawagonish Road became Ocean Westway. The highway exited in the community of Martinon. At that point, it met the twisty Westfield Road, which was originally known as the King's Highway, then Route 102, to Fredericton. The new road was nicknamed the Martinon Cut-off, as it did indeed cut off much of what was then cottage country in Martinon. It also by-passed Ketepec, Belmont, Acamac, and South Bay, but earned its nickname because it exited in Martinon. Maps refer to the cut-off as the Martinon Bypass, but locals don't!

Oh Canada!

Written by Edwin G. Nelson in about 1888 and billed as Canada's national song, "My Own Canadian Home" was inspired by the beauty he saw from the porch of a cottage at Greenhead, overlooking portions of Grand Bay and Pokiok Narrows. The song sold more than one hundred thousand copies, and at one time it was taught to schoolchildren as a patriotic anthem. Its first lines were:

Cover of the sheet music for E.G. Nelson's
My Own Canadian Home

> Though other skies
> may be as bright and
> other lands as fair
> Though charms of
> other climes invite
> my wandering foot-
> steps there.
> Yet there is one, the
> peer of all beneath
> bright heaven's dome
> Of thee I sing, O happy
> land, My own Canadian home.

Nelson, a bookstore owner in uptown Saint John, was a prolific poet, who also wrote the patriotic pieces, "Raise the Flag" in 1891, and "Canada, Land of the Free" in 1897.

Linton legacy

The Linton farmhouse was located at the foot of Manchester Avenue, just before the railway tracks. The farm was on the hillside between Manchester Avenue and Walker Brook. In 1990 Murray Linton, the original owner's son, shared the story of how the earliest vegetables in the city came from this land,

and were sold in the City Market by his dad. Murray recalled a time when Walker Brook was blocked by debris caught in the culvert under the railbed and the valley was flooded. His dad took a boat across the lake-like pond that formed to rescue his cattle. When Murray's father sold the land to the government for housing, a promise was made to name one of the streets in the area Linton Drive. Developer Tom Smith, who built the first thirty-one homes in the subdivision in 1987, was unaware of this agreement, and today the streets in the area are named Glenwood Drive and Burnside Crescent.

The province's longest power line

Supported on two thirty-one-metre (eighty-foot) towers, the power line that stretches across the lower St. John River between Acamac on the west side and Greenhead on the east is the longest stretch of unsupported power line in New Brunswick. It is almost 1 kilometre (or 0.6 miles) long. The line has come down only once, during the Groundhog Gale on February 2, 1976.

X marks the spot

In 1883, Jim Sinclair of Navy Island claimed he had a map with an *X* marking the location of treasure that Lady La

Tour and her husband hid on the West Side. He never showed the map to anyone, so the treasure may still be there. The area on the West Side that has been examined by treasure seekers most often is at Lorneville. Treasure is said to have been hidden at Frenchmen's Creek, but has never been found. A treasure hunter from Toronto brought a map and sophisticated equipment to the area in the 1930s, and managed to locate a coin or two before giving up. Though he promised to come back he never did. Spruce Lake is another area where treasure is rumoured to be buried, and of course, Partridge Island has many stories of pirates and Irish settlers who hid their wealth—even though they had none!

Tune in to your...toilet?

The five CFBC towers that originally made the signals of the city's leading station more widely available stand in a field off Sand Cove Road. Gordon Miller was responsible for maintaining the towers when Mrs. George Chittick, who lived in the house next to the field, called CFBC in the 1970s with an unusual complaint—she said that the station's broadcasts were playing through her toilet. Miller investigated and found that Mrs. Chittick's story was completely true. In fact, he said the toilet was producing sound of fairly good quality. The strange occurrence took place because two different types of metal pipes had been joined, then rusted. This created a diode, just like one that would be found in a crystal radio set. Miller was soon able to correct the problem, and Mrs. Chittick had no further transmission of CFBC through her toilet.

Buckley Pond Sailors

Parallel to the CPR line just south of Suffolk Street, a depression that filled with runoff water became known as Buckley's Pond. It was named for a neighborhood family that lived at 31 Suffolk Street. Those who built rafts of wood dragged up from Beatteay's Beach, just across the tracks, and sailed them on the pond were referred to as Buckley Pond Sailors. Few went home dry, as the most popular activity at the pond was for those on the banks to jump aboard the rafts and sink them.

Wartime housing boom

Playing in the snow outside of the typical wartime housing in Saint John West

In December 1944 the first of the wartime housing was ready for occupancy on the former millpond, which stretched from St. John Street to Rodney Street east of Ludlow Street. It was soon announced that forty more houses would be built in the area. The West Side houses had between five and seven rooms, with concrete foundations, but no basements. Acme Construction built the millpond houses, and Wartime

Housing administered the project for the first ten years. Rents were in the range of thirty-five to fifty dollars per month.

Similar projects to help returning veterans find adequate housing were undertaken at Fundy Heights, Portland Place, and in East Saint John, as the Saint John housing stock at the time was in deplorable shape. The Portland Place development was nicknamed Baby Land, because there were so many children being pushed around the neighbourhood in strollers by new mothers. People were so satisfied with these homes that some of the area's current residents, including those who first lived there as babies, have lived in their houses since 1945.

Quinton's cornfield battle

In 1778 there was a skirmish between pre-Loyalist settlers and American raiders in the area surrounding Quinton House, which still stands at 1260 Manawagonish Road. Hugh Quinton, a pre-Loyalist settler, had planted a huge cornfield on both sides of what is now Manawagonish Road. American raiders landed in Musquash, and marched up the coast to Quinton's property. Major Gilfred Studholme, appointed to build Fort Howe and defend Parrtown against attack, heard about the raiding party, and saw to it that a force of Loyal Highlanders and Nova Scotia Rangers were hidden in the Quinton cornfield. When the Yankees arrived, they walked into the trap, and faced a volley of musket shots that drove them back down the coast to their boats at Musquash. At the time, Saint John was largely controlled by Simonds, Hazen, and White, who had come to the area in 1763 to quarry the hills for lime, and cut huge pines for masts. There was never another raid after this one.

Gershon Mayes's generosity

The Mayes Medal was an award presented to the student with the highest marks at New Albert School by Gershon S. Mayes, a successful Saint John contractor. It was in the shape of a Maltese cross. The recipient's name was engraved on the clasp, while the words *Albert School* and the year appeared on the front. Mayes also presented five-dollar gold pieces to the students with highest marks at St. Patrick's School and La Tour School, according to the December 22, 1922, issue of the *Saint John Globe*. In 1884 Mayes was considered one of the city's most eligible bachelors by the members of the Leap Year Club. He was also said to be a splendid singer. He married Miss Clark in 1885. In 1935, they celebrated their golden anniversary. Mayes was still being touted as a fine singer.

Reid's Diner

Reid's Diner stood at the foot of Main Street where the railway tracks cross the intersection at Simms Corner. Charles and Mildred Reid opened the establishment in 1948. One of the most famous items on the menu was called the Chocolate 400, and students from Saint John Vocational School flocked to Reid's to enjoy this very rich chocolate drink on their way home. Reid's Diner closed in 1983.

Laughter at the Gaiety

The Gaiety Theatre opened on Main Street in 1920 as a complement (or a competitor, depending on how you look at it) to the Community Theatre, which served the Carleton area. In 1936 Les Sprague became a partner in the theatre, and was still the projectionist when it closed in 1958. In the days when the reels had to be changed halfway through the features, the children would get quite rowdy during the break. Les would have to come out of the projection booth and holler for them to quiet down so he could start the second half of the show. His request became so routine, that one day when the children were not being noisy, he came out anyway, walked to the front of the theatre, and shouted at the top of his voice, "If you kids don't quiet down, I won't show the rest of the movie." Only when his voice echoed back at him, and a volley of laughter came from the kids, did he realize there was no need to shout that day.

West Saint John's own premier, J. B. M. Baxter

John Babington Macaulay Baxter became premier of New Brunswick in 1925. Born in Saint John West in 1868, Baxter left school at age fifteen to work as a dry goods clerk. He then worked as a butcher's accountant, and a clerk in a law office. At twenty-three he ran for city council, and was defeated—but the next year he ran again and won! He served for eighteen years as a councillor. He was admitted to the bar in 1891 and built a good practice.

In 1911 he entered provincial politics, and in 1915 was appointed attorney general. In 1921 he entered federal politics as the minister of customs, and became a leading figure in the federal Conservative Party. After returning to provincial politics he became premier in 1925, then resigned in 1930 to become chief justice of the New Brunswick Supreme Court. He had a playful side, according to one storyteller who recalled that he would hide in the basement of his Dufferin Avenue home on Halloween, and when the kids rang his doorbell, he would call to them from the cellar in a ghostly voice, insisting that they come to him to get their treats. He died in 1946 and is buried in Cedar Hill Cemetery.

A peace offering to west siders

The building that is now known as the Carleton Community Centre at Duke Street and Market Place began life in 1863 as the Carleton Public Hall. The hall was built in an effort by city council to appease west siders who felt its members did not pay much attention to their needs. The builders were J. C. Littlehale and John Wilson. The construction, which cost $18,440, was paid for by the Department of Water Works and Ferries. Over time, the building served as a lock-up, health centre, school, practice hall for Carleton Cornet Band, home to the Royal Canadian Legion-Branch 2, and as the Empress Theatre, and later the Community Theatre. The hall's third-floor auditorium was used for religious services and temperance rallies.

Saint John's oldest continuously used public building, the Carleton Community Centre, was built in 1863

Touring theatrical companies gave presentations there, including Hayward's Great Comic and Musical Entertainment, which was staged on December 18, 1872. The building is still standing—though it was destroyed by fire in 1925, it was rebuilt!

An unwelcome addition

That the west side once had a tunnel is surely a surprise to many, even those who now work in the Irving Pulp Mill where the tunnel was built during one of its many expansions. American engineer Edward Sheehan was hired by mill owner K. C. Irving, to oversee the expansion, and one of the conditions of his work was that the mill had to keep production going during the renovations. To meet that objective, Sheehan designed a tunnel for the trains that ran into the mill to pick up product. When Irving came to inspect the ongoing expansion, he thought the tunnel an unnecessary expense, and referred to it in a derogatory tone as Sheehan's Tunnel. He continued to do so as long as it existed, as whenever he saw it, it was a fresh reminder of money that had gone out of his pocket to construct it. Eventually, with other expansions and changes the tunnel disappeared. No one at the mill today knows the term, but for a while in the 1960s, Saint John West had a tunnel. The full story can be read in Doug How and Ralph Costello's book *K. C.—The Biography of K. C. Irving*.

Chittick's honour

George Corbett Chittick (1904–1973) operated a successful construction business on Saint John's West Side throughout his adult years. Some of Chittick's projects are still in existence, including Thorne's Hardware on Chesley Drive, and the first four-lane highway west of Saint John, which runs from Spruce Lake to Musquash. He was appointed a Freeman of Saint John in 1958, and was an honourary lifetime member of the Fire Chiefs Association for helping to rescue Saint John firefighter John Kyle, who was trapped for four hours when a blazing building on Main Street collapsed on him. Chittick's middle name, Corbett, was chosen to honour the doctor who brought him into the world, as he risked his life travelling to Musquash in a snowstorm to aid George's mother during his birth.

A berry special train

The Grand Southern Railway was built to connect Saint John West to St. Stephen, located 141 kilometres (88 miles) away, in 1882. The line was not a money-maker, and was sold to CPR in 1911. The company was given a 999-year lease. In 1935, CPR closed a section of the line between Bonny River-St. George and St. Stephen. It also cut service from St. George to Saint John to three times a week, and eventually, in 1988, this service was abandoned altogether. In the 1950s, it was popular for Saint Johners to take the train to Prince of Wales, Lepreau, or Pennfield, on berry-picking outings, thus the train was nicknamed the Blueberry Special. At the time it moved so slowly that it was said a picker could get off the front of the train, pick a pail of berries, and jump back on the end of the train before it passed by.

Like a rock

Red Granite Works, managed by F. T. C. Burpee, was situated on Union Street near the railway crossing at St. John Street. Using pink granite brought to the site from quarries in St. George, the company turned rough pieces of rock into shafts, monuments, and decorative works. The company's products were exported by rail primarily to central Canada and the mid-western United States, including the granite used for the State House in Albany, New York. The firm employed fifty-five men at its cutting, shaping, and polishing operation. Burpee lamented that only one day's work a month was done for New Brunswick businesses because Scottish manufacturers had such a grip on the local market.

A fountain for all

The Band of Mercy Fountain was placed at the head of Rodney Wharf in 1893 by an organization that was much like our Animal Rescue League today. The fountain featured a five- to six-foot-tall bronze figure of Hebe, the Greek goddess. The granite base had water spouts for horses, dogs, and humans to drink from. The statue was imported by T. McAvity and Sons, with Mr. Sleeth and Mr. Quinlan doing the local granite work and putting the fountain into position. In the 1960s, it was moved to Tilley Square opposite the Carleton Community Centre. The fountain is no longer operating, but children in the area refer to the drinking bowl that horses once used as the "bird bath."

Chicken tricks

Willard Moore used the motto, "No cheap service, just service cheap" to promote his meat and grocery business at the corner of Main and Walnut streets until 1965. The Bank of Nova Scotia now stands where Moore's grocery was located. The most famous Willard Moore story begins with a complaint from a lady who was not satisfied with the only chicken Moore had in his shop late one Saturday. So he took the chicken out back, stuck his hand in the crevice, fluffed it up, and took it back to show her. He held it up and asked, "Would this chicken would be better?" She replied, "It's still not big enough—so I will take both of them."

A century of curling

Though the Carleton Curling Club was founded in 1895, the group did not lease a clubhouse until 1908, so it must be assumed that its members played the game outdoors, possibly on the skating rink at the old millpond on St. John Street. Women did not join the club until the 1930s. The female members stopped curling during World War Two, and resumed in the 1950s, though even then the club did not install separate washrooms for the women's comfort. The ice at the club was all natural until January 15, 1949, when C. C. Bradley, president, tossed the first stone to open a new era of more reliable curling on artificial ice.

The name game

Ken Meating has not one but three nicknames. He is called King Fisher by the fishermen at Dominion Park

King Fisher Ken Meating with his smallest smelt of the season

because of his prowess in catching smelt. He pulled 2,424 out of the river in 2007. When he goes to the Legion they call him Deacon, as he is a lay reader at St. George's Church. Thirdly, and for the same reason, he is referred to as Monsignor when he visits the Tim Hortons where west siders gather. Among their discussions are the many nicknames for area residents. The West Side was a particularly prolific place for nicknames, and many were derived from the railroad and port operations; however, as far as can be discerned, only Ken Meating has three.

Lou Murphy's Bridge

The overpass on Greenhead Road that spans the CPR line from Fairville to South Bay is known as Gifford Bridge or Lou Murphy's Bridge. The marshalling yards where trains would be assembled were located here, and the trains often blocked the only road to Milford and Randolph. Two of the Gifford family's children died in a fire when equipment could not get to the conflagration. In 1984, after much agitation, a bridge was finally built over the tracks. It was named after Lou Murphy, the local MLA who had campaigned hard for the bridge. The approaches to the bridge were wider than necessary, so that two lanes could be added as business in the area grew. The additional lanes were never constructed, and in 2005 Moosehead Breweries, J. D. Irving Ltd., and the City of Saint John planted maple trees along the unused portion of the roadway and landscaped the area.

A hall for the Prentice Boys

The cornerstone for the King Edward Lodge was laid at 105 Guilford Street West on October 19, 1906. The Carleton Cornet Band played at the ceremony, and lodge members paraded through the streets along with members of brother and sister organizations. The day was one to be remembered, and the building was scheduled for completion by the "end of the month." In August 1947 the Protestant Association of Prentice Boys placed a memorial stone to honour departed members in Cedar Hill Cemetery. It is one of the most imposing stones at the Lancaster Avenue location, and was erected under the direction of the then-president Garfield Melvin. Melvin continued his association with the Prentice Boys until they ceased operation in 1977. The organization's hall on Guilford Street was converted to apartments and still stands today.

A beautiful tribute

The Eliza McIntosh Memorial is possibly the finest stone in Cedar Hill Cemetery. Carved into the grey granite is the life-size figure of an angel with the most serene face. There is not another stone like it in the cemetery. The original owners of the stone were having it shipped from Italy to Ontario, but would not pay the freight to Central Canada after it arrived in Saint John. The stone was put in storage at a West Side Pier, and sold at auction to the McIntosh family, who bought it to honour their mother, Eliza. The McIntosh family was in the cartage business, and easily moved the stone to its central position in the cemetery. With the exception of her son Joseph, who remained in New Brunswick, Eliza McIntosh's children dispersed to various areas of Canada.

Grand Manan's lobster cans

In 1823, Dr. Henry Cook and his younger brother, John, arrived in Saint John. Henry practised medicine in the city, while John opened a drugstore, or apothecary. Henry died at the age of forty-eight in 1844. When John's drugstore burned in 1858 he moved to Grand Manan, where he established the island's first lobster-canning operation on the Thoroughfare. He later returned to Carleton and re-established his drugstore business. His son, also named John, continued his father's interest and owned lobster canning plants throughout the Maritimes.

Five Fathom Hole

Five Fathom Hole is found on the Musquash River as it enters Musquash Harbour at the south end of Five Fathom Road. The name suggests that the depth of the water in the hole is nine metres (thirty feet), as a fathom is about two metres (six feet)—the measurement was originally based on the length of a man's outstretched arms. Tide charts of the area show eight- to ten-metre (twenty-six- to thirty-foot) tides in the area between the east and west banks. This is the deepest area before Musquash Head, which is twenty-four kilometres (thirteen sea miles) downstream. A ferry once operated at this location, linking the road south along the coast from Saint John to Dipper Harbour.

Tribute to a master

In 1925, at sixty-nine years of age, Stanley Olive started the 21st St. George's Scout Troop. He was also active with the 5th St. Jude's Troop. At that time he could still lead a twenty-kilometre (twelve-mile) hike from the hall at St. George's to Spruce Lake. When Olive died in Saint John West on February 2, 1937, he was the oldest scoutmaster in the British Empire. Shortly after Olive's death, Robert Dole began a fund to erect a suitable memorial to his friend. Dole received permission from the family of artist Ernest S. Carlos (who had died in World War One) to make an authentic copy of his painting, *The Pathfinder*. The painting depicts Jesus looking over the shoulder of a Scout planning a journey. The image was rendered in glass by the famed McCausland Company of Toronto, and placed in St. George's Church on Sunday, November 9, 1941. It was unveiled by Dole, and dedicated by Canon W. P. Haigh, and an address was given by former premier and west sider, J. B. M. Baxter.

Pirates of Saint John

In 1837, a group of west siders who lived in the valley be-tween the Blue Rock (St. James Street) and Courtenay Hill (Duke Street), rowed across the harbour, and helped themselves to the furnishings and goods central Saint Johners had placed in boats for safekeeping during a great fire that threatened the central city. The goods were supposedly rowed over to safety in Saint John West by the west siders. The items were never returned, and central Saint Johners, who likened the incident to the Algerian pirate raids on Ireland, nicknamed the west siders "Algreens" or "Algerines." Though the name has now all but disappeared, as late as 2001 there was still an Algerine Bridge Club operating. Peter Murphy, Frank O'Brien, and Anna Kinsella shared this information.

He didn't feel a thing

On January 21, 1847, Dr. Martin Hunter Peters was the first to administer ether anesthetic to a patient in British North America. Peters then performed an operation on the pa-tient, who was rendered insensible by inhaling the vapour com-pound. Following the surgery, a little cold water to the fore-head was used to revive the patient. He said he had "been very happy and quite unconscious and did not feel anything." The Peters' house where the operation was performed still stands at the southeast corner of Guilford and Watson streets. Foster Hammond was the owner until 2008, and would often regale those passing by with the story. An account of the operation was written up in a paper by Dr. Joseph A. MacDougall in the *Canadian Journal of Anesthesia* in September 1987, and there was no dispute with regard to the claim of Peters' first.

Blue Rockers

Those who lived on the rocky outcrop bounded by Victoria, Queen, St. James, and Albert streets were nicknamed Blue Rockers. The area, which overlooks the port and rail yard, is about thirty metres (one hundred feet) above street level at its highest point. During World War Two, the cliff was used as an observation area. In the 1950s ten families lived in five houses on the outcrop. Among those living there was Fran Cuppens, a famed stained glass artist. He is said to have filled every window of a former army hut with stained glass as he developed his skill. At the edge of the hill, the Clark family lived on the corner of Albert and St. James. They made lemon extract and exported it all over Canada from the Blue Rock.

The view of the harbour from Blue Rock

A potato phantom

A murder occurred in the area where the Blue Rocks are washed by the tides of Saint John Harbour, in the place where Pier 14 was later built. The shed on the pier was used to store potatoes being shipped to Cuba and other southern destinations. They would be stacked on pallets about two metres (six feet) high. The men moving the pallets to the ship for loading would sometimes see a wispy figure of a man darting between them as they approached with a forklift. No one ever found a real human being walking among the potatoes, so the apparition became known as the Potato Shed Ghost. This story was conveyed by Basil Hamilton, whose home stood on City Line overlooking this shed.

No livestock in these barns

Saint John's car barns had nothing to do with vehicles as most people think of them today. Car barn was the nickname given to the garages where streetcars were repaired and maintained. Streetcars were the first mechanical mass-movers of people in Saint John. The first streetcar line in Carleton opened on June 23, 1906. A maintenance barn for the streetcars was built on a wharf extending from Union Street at Duke Street. In 1931, when the port expanded, and the Millpond was filled in, a new barn was built on Tower Street at Ludlow Street. In 1948, the city's first buses were secretly stored there prior to streetcar service ending. The building served as a depot for

Speedway Transport until 1957, when they moved to Molson Avenue. The Tower Street building was then razed, and a labour hall was built in its place. The Molson Avenue Speedway site was torn down, and is now housing, originally built in 1977 by Manford Thompson, and known as Thompson Place.

Property of the king

The king's arrowhead was a symbol used by King George III's men to designate ownership of land and goods. This included giant pines designated for use as masts on ships in the King's Navy, even if they were on private lands. The symbol can be seen today on old cannons and chiselled into solid chunks of grey granite used as boundary markers, such as those on the corners of the property where Martello Tower stands.

No ordinary secretary

After Lancaster became a city in 1953, the police found themselves with no police matron. When a female had to be escorted by the police, they would use the services of the City of Saint John's matron; however, she was not always available to help out in Lancaster, and when she did work in Lancaster, the city was charged by Saint John for her services. The Lancaster Police offices were located in city hall, where Ruth Brittain was the secretary. It was suggested that Ruth become the police matron. She was paid $1,200 a year, and was usually called upon about three or four times a month. When Lancaster amalgamated with Saint John in 1967, Ruth was no longer needed; thus, she goes down in history as the first and only police matron in the city of Lancaster. The Brittain family still has Ruth's badge as proof of her unique position.

Ridgewood Golf Course

Ridgewood Golf Course was developed in a former farmer's field at the north side of the CPR line at Boggs Crossing at South Bay. The nine-hole course opened around 1920, and closed fifteen years later, when the main lodge was destroyed by fire. The

The golfers of Ridgewood in the 1930s

course reopened in 1936, and a new lodge was constructed at that time. The tower on the south end of the clubhouse was topped by a golf-club weathervane, which clearly identified the building's use, and remains on the building to this day. The Ridgewood Golf Course also had a caddy house. Sid Lingart was the pro at the club, and he advertised his services in the paper in 1936. The lodge that was constructed in 1936 is still being used by the Ridgewood Rehabilitation Centre today.

The strength of Reverend Wood

When Reverend Abraham Wood was curate (or assist-ant minister) of uptown Trinity Church, he was rowed across the harbour to minister to Anglicans at the Chapel of Ease that stood on the upper block of King Street West. This continued until St. George's Church opened on November 6, 1821. Wood wrote poems and painted; some of his artistic work is still extant, though held in a private collection.

An incident that occurred when Wood was at Otty's Mill on Straight Shore demonstrated that he was a powerful man. Wood got his coat caught in the wheel of the mill—but had such strength that though the machine tore off half his coat, sleeve and all, he was not harmed. He later moved to Grand Lake to serve a parish. Wood was living on Charlotte Street at the time of the Great Fire in Saint John in 1877, and lost all of his possessions. He was eighty-six years of age at that time and had to start again.

One bachelor down, two to go

In 1884, the *Saint John Globe* published a list of the city's most eligible bachelors, as selected by the Leap Year Club. The list named several west siders, including John Ring, who the club said "should have someone at the door when he gets back to Carleton after the Post Office closes;" Alban F. Emery, the assistant principal of the Albert School in Carleton, who was described as socially active, but "timid of the other sex;" and Gershon Mayes, described as a "government contractor, believed to be making money fast."

Of the three, we know that Mayes did marry one Miss Clark on February 12, 1885, at St. Jude's Church, on a day so stormy many guests could not get to the ceremony. In fact, the weather was so terrible that the newlyweds weren't able to get away on their honeymoon.

Lancaster on the big screen

The El Belgrano Lodge and Restaurant on the outskirts of Lancaster was a stylish spot for dining and dancing from the time it opened in 1946 until it closed in 1980. At the time of the restaurant's opening, Highway 1 was the gateway to the city from Maine and other American destinations, and American visitors were attracted to the modern-looking property, which was not unlike something they would see at home. In 1986, the lodge was used as the location for a dance scene in *Children of a Lesser God*, the made-in-Saint John movie that starred William Hurt and Marlee Matlin, and won several Academy Awards the following year.

Saint John's first mayor

Gabriel G. Ludlow was the city's first mayor. Though the house he lived in is no longer standing there is speculation that the building that now stands in its place at 180 Duke Street was built on the original home's foundation. He made a partial payment for a pew at St. George's Church before it was constructed just west and uphill from his house, but as the church did not open until November 6, 1821, and Ludlow died in 1808, he never had the chance to sit in it.

Ludlow was buried in the Carleton Cemetery, but his plot was covered over when the new Carleton-Kirk United Church was built in 1976. Before doing so, the church removed all of the stones from what was an unkempt cemetery and placed them in the courtyard of the new church. Ludlow's stone can still be read. It tells us that the leader of New Brunswick was once called the president, rather than the premier. His wife, Anne, is described on the stone as a "relict," which simply meant she was his widow.

Mayor of Murphyville

Lou Murphy was called the Mayor of Murphyville, a name he placed over the door of his house on Milford Road. Lou created an attraction on the hill next to his home, which he called Thunder Hill. It features models of homes he admired, the church he attended, St. Rose of Lima, and other religious figures. Lou served on the school board, as a city councillor, and

Lou Murphy, mayor of Murphyville, at the Gabriel G. Ludlow Commemorating Day in 1983

as a member of the legislative assembly, but still found time to champion many causes, including the losing battle to have the tolls removed from the Harbour Bridge after it opened in 1968. He was the published author of three books of poems, anecdotal witticisms, and inspirations, which were enjoyed by and inspired many people. Cases of his books were found after his death, and have since been distributed throughout schools in the Maritimes courtesy of Lou's nephew, Donnie Coholan. Donnie also maintains the Thunder Hill attraction, and makes sure it is lit up at Christmas.

Good times
on the Golden Mile

The Golden Mile was the nickname given to Fairville Boulevard, which runs west from Simms Corner to the heights of Manawagonish Road near the Cedar Hill Cemetery extension, when business boomed along the street in the 1950s and 1960s. Initially, the street was built by the City of Lancaster to get ever-increasing loads of traffic off Main Street and Manawagonish Road. In 1959 Kelly Tire, Canadian Pittsburg Industries, and Western Wire and Cable opened on Fairville Boulevard. By 1964 Canadian General Electric, Kimberly Clark, Saint John Tile and Terrazzo, T. S. Simms, Day and Ross, and Robert Morse followed. The flourish of activity by local and out-of-town interests led to the nickname.

The Roll 'n' Shake Restaurant, built at the top of the hill in 1964, was as good a reason as any to drive the Golden Mile. The Fundy Drive-In was located just across from the restaurant. The outdoor theatre was nicknamed the Foggy Drive-In because prevailing winds off the bay blew in the misty fog that often interrupted the shows for those who were watching—some people, of course, had other things on their minds at the drive-in!

Fit for a saint

The sand berm and beach leading across Manawagonish Marsh to the Irving Nature Park is known as Saint's Rest, a name that is frequently questioned. There are three theories regarding how the beach got its name. The first is that a ship named after a saint was shipwrecked there. The second is that the area was given the name because it is adjacent to two graveyards—Holy Cross and Greenwood—where many "saints" are buried. The last explanation is that a house of entertainment existed there a century ago, and when well-known West Side personalities arrived there for their relaxation, their entrance was announced as "the saints have come" or the "saints are at the C."

It is believed that Saint's Rest was marshland until 1869, when the Saxby Gale changed the Fundy coast forever. During the gale, tides were three metres (ten feet) higher than usual, which caused the edge of the marsh to fill with sand. This change proved beneficial, as today 280,000 people cross the beach every year to reach the magnificent walking trails at the Irving Nature Park.

Woes over West Side water

In 1854 the city appointed Reverend Frederick Coster as chairman of a commission working to bring water from Spruce Lake ten kilometres (six miles) west of the city to the lower West Side. The project was completed in 1859 at a cost of ninety-two thousand dollars. It consisted of a main line that resembled a stovepipe lined with cement. Edward W. Serrell, who built the successful suspension bridge at the Reversing Falls in 1853, and William Beard of Brooklyn, New York, laid the pipe. Serrell dropped out of the project and Beard finished it. The pipe, known as Bull's Patent Indestructible Cement Pipe, was guaranteed for twenty-five years—and some portions lasted almost a century! It is said that taxes needed to pay for the job made Reverend Coster so unpopular with the people of Carleton that he had to have his wardens or vestrymen accompany him on his ecclesiastical duties thereafter.

Rocky Road to Dublin

K aren Farthing has a drawing of a set of steps that her great-grandfather was hired to construct from Tilton's Corner to the summer resort at the mouth of the Reversing Falls. This resort would have been Hamilton's Hill, which Richard Avery ran before 1848. The sketch clearly shows Prince Street, Tilton's Corner, and half a kilometer of walkways leading to what he marked as the summer resort at the Reversing Falls. He notes that the walkway is "about the crookest road I ever travelled," and he has nicknamed it the Rocky Road to Dublin.

The (beach) house that Jack built

S ans Souci on the Bay was the name David Russell Jack gave to a cluster of fourteen cottages he built on Sand Cove Road overlooking Duck Cove. He operated the cottages for tourists (many from the United States) from 1907 until his death in 1914. The cottages had a private beach, a tennis court, and a library where shows were presented in the evenings. In 2005 the library building still stood, though it had been modernized, and the tennis court was still there. All property owners in the area have rights to the private beach. Though the beach houses Jack built are not readily seen, some have been modernized and are still being lived in.

Building benevolence

Dexter Construction was one of the leading road-building firms in the province from around 1930 to 1960. It had its main office and equipment garage on Dever Road. The firm is gone, but the buildings it once used still stand. Dexter Construction was formed when road building began in earnest with the introduction of automobiles late in the second decade of the twentieth century. Principal members of the company included Cecil, Russell S., and Donald Dexter. One of the company's legacies is St. Mark's Church, located just across from their Dever Road operations in Greendale. The church benefitted greatly from the Dexter family's benevolence when it was constructed in the early 1960s. Dexter Construction was sold in 1975.

A day at the beach

Dominion Park was, and is, the only place for west siders to swim in fresh water when fog shrouds the Fundy. The park is nestled in a north-facing cove on Greenhead Island at the end of Dominion Park Road, about two kilometres from Main Street and Church Avenue. Originally known as Rayne's Beach, the area was renamed Dominion Park by the county council of Saint John on July 1, 1945. Red Chase was the caretaker at the park for many years, and lived in the Tippett Cottage at the east end of the beach. The canteen and dance hall stood on posts near the middle of the beach. The building burned

Aerial view of Dominion Park in 1972

in the 1980s, and was replaced by the canteen, washroom, and lifeguard service area that stands in the park today. A maintenance shed was built just south of where Tippett Cottage stood, and it serves as headquarters for the summer-only caretaker today. In 1946, eight hundred people daily was typical summer attendance, and buses travelling to the beach from Simm's Corner were packed on every trip.

Union Point School

Union Point School began operating as early as 1850, when the area was part of Assumption Parish on the lower West Side. It served as both school and mission house for what was to become St. Rose Parish in Fairville, Randolph, and Milford. In

1871, the public school system took over the operation of Union Point School. When Union Point School burnt on March 2, 1961, it was owned by the Irvings who intended to expand their pulp mill onto the property. They bought the school when it closed in May 1960, as the new St. Rose School opened.

A murderous tale

Come now my friend and lend an ear
A dreadful story you shall hear
This murderous deed was done of late
In eighteen hundred and sixty-eight.

This "come ye all" goes on to recount the courtship of west sider Sarah Margaret Vail, which began when she met architect John Monroe as he oversaw construction of the Masonic Lodge on the corner of Charlotte and Lancaster streets.

One of their favourite meeting spots was the McCarthy Grounds at the Bay Shore. Behind Loch Lomond, John Monroe shot Sarah Margaret Vail and her baby, Ella Mae Monroe, the product of their illicit tryst. Sarah does not haunt the West Side, but her ghost has been seen in the woodland beyond the airport.

Ghosts that haunt
the West Side

There are at least sixteen sites on the West Side where ghost sightings have been reported. They are:

- Navy Island—The ghosts of Charnisay, headless men, and Lady La Tour haunt the island.
- Harbour Bridge Toll Plaza—The ghost of Daniel Keymore is seen.
- Market Place (First Trainor House)—A suicide victim moans in a hallway after midnight.
- Queen Street (Second Trainor House)—A deceased family member walks through the TV room during the nightly news.
- DeMonts Street—The ghost of Mr. Splane shovels coal in the basement on cold, cold nights.
- Biermann House on Lancaster Avenue—A headless lady rocks all night in the front bedroom.
- Martello Tower—The ghost of a British soldier picks berries on the hillside, chains rattle in dungeon area, and moans are heard.
- Assumption Church on Dufferin Row—A dead man led an unemployed lady to his widow who was working in the rectory. The widow needed a helper, and presumably the dead man thought she may give the unemployed woman a job.
- St. Jude's Church on Lancaster Street—Deceased members of the church's sewing circle have been seen and heard upstairs, especially by young people; but when the youngsters alert their elders, the adults are unable to see or hear the ghosts.

- Jewett Castle—A shifting shadow known as the Shade of Jewett annoyed the hospital staff that he believes have desecrated his formerly glorious home.
- Fence at the corner of City Line and Tower Street—A ragged woman believed to have been a nun or teacher at a nearby convent appears by the fence.
- Peter's House on Guilford at Watson Street—Many disturbances have been reported at this house—a cat that plays piano, rooms that suddenly cool off, dogs moan at nothing, a rattling sound comes from the walls.
- Partridge Island—British redcoats appear, and Irishmen who died in the famine roam the property.
- Shortcut between Lancaster Avenue and City Line—A berry picker was spooked by a Victorian gentleman who was watching her, but he then disappeared.
- Shed 13—The potato shed ghost, who is believed to have been a murder victim, floats around behind the stacks of potatoes. Some brave longshoremen, afraid of the ghost, would not work on the property.
- Various locations—The ghost of Lady La Tour. Traditionally, West Side children were told that the ghost of Françoise Marie Jacquelin La Tour, who died of a broken heart while defending Fort La Tour in 1645, roamed the area looking for kids out beyond their curfews. Until the late 1950s most Saint Johners believed Fort La Tour was on the west side of the harbour (near the present-day Harbour Bridge Plaza), so it was natural that her ghost would appear on that side of the city. After all, a school named after Lady La Tour was located in their part of town, and the particularly thick West Side fog would be especially attractive for a ghost. To this day folks still see

a wispy figure in a long grey gown gliding about the area from time to time.

Pieces of Montreal

The Vale was the name given to the valley between Manawagonish Road on the north and Crow's Mountain on the south. The Vale was largely farmland until the end of World War Two. When the war ended a Montreal developer saw potential in the area for a subdivision; the result is a number of streets with names from his hometown, like Montreal Avenue, and Sherbrooke and Catherwood streets.

Mosquito Cove

While many areas of West Saint John may seem like they deserve to be called Mosquito Cove, only one area has officially been given this name. Mosquito Cove is located where Greenhead Road crosses a channel of the St. John River that separates Greenhead Island from West Saint John. This canal was originally dug out so logs from the South Bay mills could be floated more directly into the Pokiok Narrows, and then through the Reversing Falls to mills that lined both sides of the Straight Shore. The Mosquito Cove area was also known as Kingsville, and one of its most famed residents was Bartlett Lingley, who ran a lumber mill there for many years. Upon making his fortune he moved to the United States, where he died at age sixty on September 21, 1881, in far off San Francisco.

The Paris Crew

All four members of the Paris Crew are buried in Cedar Hill Cemetery. Against all odds, this group of fishermen from Saint John West beat the best European rowing crews at their own game in Paris in 1867. They were Samuel Hutton, Elijah Ross, George Price, and Robert Fulton. Hutton died in a sailing accident off Manawagonish Island when the vessel *Primrose* went to the bottom during a race on August 21, 1894. Because Hutton's body was not found until October many believed his remains were never interred, and did not lie under the prominent marker in the cemetery; however, a member of Hutton's family dispelled this myth. This family member also said that some of Hutton's possessions are now owned by Joe Tippett, a resident of Moncton. Among the items is the watch Hutton owned, which was given to Joe's dad by Sam's widow when he went to university.

Quarry commotion

Bald Hill is the name given to what was once a forested area between the railway line north of Dever Road and the St. John River. The wooded hill was a seldom-visited spot until it was bought by the Irvings, and became the site of a controversial quarrying operation. Unfortunately, blasting at the quarry sometimes disturbs the site's neighbours. In 2005 the company forgot to issue a voluntary thirty-day notification to people living in the area, and a blasting event on March 18 took neighbours of the hill by surprise. Irving-owned Gulf Operators issued an apology and the quarrying continues to this day.

For the birds

The thick spruce woodlands bounded by Seawood Lane and Fisherman's Road have long been known as Crow's Mountain because of the crows that congregate there. The area has changed dramatically in the last fifty years—the summer cottages that were scattered through the woods are now year-round residences, and new, larger homes have been built on the hill—but the crows still love the area, and the name still fits.

Lancaster's sweetheart

Some poor fellow had it bad when he wrote the poem about his "Sweet Zella of Lancaster Heights." Unfortunately, he did not reveal his own identity or his beloved's last name, so we cannot trace this story to see if a successful courtship took place on the hills overlooking Saint John West, perhaps around Martello Tower. The poem was published in the *Saint John Globe* on September 30, 1893.

> Mid fashions' bright circles I've met
> In art's richest costumes attir'd
> The brown and blond beauty
> And dark brown'd brunette

And each lovely type have admired;
But tho' there are charmers seductive and fair
Amongst these frail lady like sprites
For beauty and style and grace none compare
With Zella of Lancaster Heights.
My Zella, Fair Zella,
For beauty and style and grace none compare
With Zella of Lancaster Heights

Save our salmon!

The *Daily Globe* of October 31, 1893, gives details of the Carleton Salmon Hatchery, the first attempt to ensure that the mighty salmon would continue to thrive in the St. John River despite the fact that it was being polluted by city sewage and waste wood from lumber mills. The fish pond was located in the old Tidal Mill of Carleton. It was reported that two hundred thousand eggs were taken from the fish pond, which could hold a thousand fish for the purpose of milting them. Fish had been kept in perfect condition in the pond for up to two years, the report stated. The fish had been caught in seine nets in the upper river at Grand Falls. Charles McCluskey and Alexander Mowatt were mentioned as two principals involved in the operation.

Slippery business

At Spruce Lake, men from Lorneville found winter work cutting blocks of ice to augment their summer trade of salmon fishing. Several ice houses were located on the south side of the lake, about 1.6 kilometres (1 mile) from the east-end dam. William Scully was the owner of the business. Ice was delivered to homes through Fairville and Saint John West. The railways were big users of crushed ice, too, and there was a spur line in that area to make it easier to move the ice. One local entrepreneur, Melvin McCavour, shipped fresh-caught salmon packed in Spruce Lake ice to New York City, timing the delivery to Saint John's Union Station so the fish would arrive in New York the next day before the ice had melted.

Final resting place of Saint John's elite

Cedar Hill Cemetery on Lancaster Avenue overlooking the Reversing Falls opened in 1792, and when the cemetery began to get full, the Cedar Hill Extension on Manawagonish Road was opened in 1922. In 1968 the company also took over Greenwood Cemetery on Sand Cove Road, which was established in 1869. While all three cemeteries contain interesting stones, Cedar Hill is where people like Charles Gorman, and Paris Crew members Robert Fulton, Elijah Ross, George Price, and Sam Hutton, along with their manager James A. Harding are buried. In addition, the only provincial premier from West Saint John, J. B. M. Baxter, is buried there, as is the man who brought water to Saint John West, Frederick Coster.

Cedar Hill is the also the only cemetery in town in which a judge held court. While the exact date is unknown, a citation in John K. C. Willett's scrapbook #83, page 14, tells the story of how Magistrate Allingham resorted to using the tool shed at Cedar Hill as the location for his proceedings when his courtroom in Fairville was destroyed by fire on May 1, 1922. The judge used the shed for a few weeks before moving his court to the Temperance Hall in Fairville.

The West Side ferries, from beginning to end

From April 13, 1789, to June 30, 1953, the City of Saint John supported a ferry link from the Sand Point, Rodney Slip, in Saint John West to the foot of Princess Street in central Saint John. Until 1853, the ferry was the only way to get to town (as Saint John was referred to). From 1789 to 1839, simple rowboats were used as the ferries on the route. The steamboat *Victoria* was added in 1839, and the *Lady Colebrooke* was added to the run on September 30, 1841. On August 3, 1860, the *Prince of Wales* (named for the prince who visited that year) began its service, and ran until 1869. The *Ouangondy* and *Western Extension* were both operated from July 13, 1870, until 1905, though they were kept in dock until 1908 for emergency use. The *Ludlow* and the *Governor Carleton* made the trip from July 6, 1905, to April 1933.

The last ferry on the route was the *Loyalist*.

The ferries generally provided reliable service, but they were expensive to build and operate, and at times squabbles at common council over repairs to docks or vessels disrupted service. There were also times when the ferry could not operate as usual, due to ice floes moving down the river in winter, or freshet conditions creating stronger than normal tides in spring. Sometimes, the movements of deep-sea vessels in the harbour created problems for the ferries, too.

Passenger numbers dropped following World War Two, as increasing prosperity allowed more and more people to buy cars. The situation came to a head in June 1953, when the deficit for the previous year was disclosed—it was $70,000, and it would take more than $112,000 to make the repairs to the wharves necessary to keep the service running. In addition, a certificate to operate the ailing ferry could not be procured from the Department of Transport. The ferry service ended on June 30, 1953.

Carleton Union Lodge

The Carleton Union Lodge at the corner of Lancaster and Charlotte streets was established by the Masons by warrant from Great Britain in 1846. Prior to that time, meetings of the lodge were held in private homes at Dykeman's Corner, Lambert's Hall, and Cornfield's Hall on King Street. In 1867 the Carleton Union Lodge united with other lodges to become the 8 Grand Lodge of New Brunswick. In 1870 the current hall was opened by M. W. G. M. B. L. Peters and has since served as the base for Masonic activity in Saint John West.

Cassie Hassie's Wilderness

According to Sharon Justason, one home in the small scattering of houses in the area around Havelock School–Seawood School and Seaside Park belonged to an old lady named Cassie Hassie in the 1920s. She became demented as the years passed, and the children of the area were frightened of her. They avoided the area and referred to it as Cassie Hassie's Wilderness.

The line that divides

City Line, which runs from south to north from Fort Dufferin to Duke Street, was originally the dividing line between West Saint John and Lancaster. The names of streets that crossed City Line changed on its west side—Charlotte Street became Charlotte Street Extension, Tower Street became Martello Row, and St. John Street changed to Dufferin Row. Street numbers in the area are mixed up to this day, as they were issued by two separate governing bodies, the city councils of Saint John and Lancaster.

Boggs Crossing

The Boggs Crossing underpass is located where the CPR line crossed the King's Highway—the tracks are now owned by NB Southern Railway, and the highway is now called Manchester Avenue. The crossing was named after a Colonel Boggs who lived on the highest point of land on Manchester Avenue. Boggs's next-door neighbour, Edis Flewelling, claimed that he was buried there, though no marker exists. Before the present subway was built, the crossing was the scene of many fatal accidents. The first passenger train crossed the subway on October 19, 1960, while travelling from Saint John to Montreal.

Shag Rocks

From Sea Street at Bay Shore a low ledge of rough rock, known as the Shag Rocks, can be seen about half a kilometre (a third of a mile) offshore. The ledge runs roughly parallel with Partridge Island, to its left and Thrumcap and Manawagonish (or Mahogany) Island to its right. These rocky ledges and islands were once the edge of Saint John West before the sea wore the shoreline to where it is today. The Shag Rocks may have gotten their name from their ruggedness. They were used for target practice by the artillery at Fort Dufferin in the late nineteenth century. Shag is also a nickname for the cormorants that frequent the area in spring and summer. The birds do not nest on the rocks as they are underwater at high tide. It was off the Shag Rocks that Daniel Keymore drowned in 1889 when his boat was swamped by a rogue wave. He is now known as the ghost of West Saint John.

The gift of sanctuary

S mith's Bird Sanctuary consists of six hectares (fourteen acres) of heavily forested hillside in a triangular patch bordered by Edgehill Row, Pipeline Road, and Manchester Avenue. Carl Smith donated the land for the sanctuary, including a portion of his backyard. The birds, deer, rabbits, skunks, raccoons, and porcupines have certainly enjoyed his gift. Until a housing development was recently constructed on the west edge of the sanctuary, only a few neighbours knew of it, and had wandered among the 150-year-old spruce trees that survived cutting by those who farmed the nearby valley. The trees were growing on such a steep incline that cutting them down was next to impossible.

Donovan's green piece

D onovan's Boulevard is located at the west end of Queen Street, which is the widest street in Saint John West. Two grassy plots were built up in the centre of the street and form a green-belt extension to Queen Square. They were a gift from Simon P. Donovan to the city in perpetuity. Donovan's butcher shop stood at 203–205 Queen Street. He did a lively trade with the ships that came into the harbour all winter in the days before the St. Lawrence Seaway opened in 1959. During repairs to a waterline under the grass in the 1980s the city proposed paving the plots over. Those that knew of Donovan's gift protested to the city, and the plots were left as a green space in memory of "Bouch" Donovan.

Gilfred rides again

Gilford Street West was named after Major Gilfred Studholme; somehow his name was copied incorrectly and the error perpetuated. Studholme was sent to Saint John and stationed at Fort Howe to help the Loyalists of 1783 settle in their new community, known then as Parrtown. Studholme eventually left the area and moved to Apohaqui, where he became a gentleman farmer. Tradition says he buried his gold in a field overlooking the Kennebecasis, and that now his ghost swoops down on a big white horse to scare off anyone who tries to take it. Another story says a local farmer got some of the gold and built a beautiful house on the property as proof of his find. A plaque atop Fort Howe in his memory is worth reading—and spells Gilfred's name correctly.

Brazilian bird feeders

It might seem strange to see the Brazilian bird feeders that are located in the Irving Nature Park. An anonymous seafarer donated at least four of the feeders to the park between 2002 and 2005. They are made from China fir, or Cunninghamia, taken from Castanheiras Park in São Paulo, Brazil. William Hering has grown hundreds of Cunninghamia trees over the past fifty-five years, in an effort to contribute to the reforestation of the 133-hectare (330-acre) park. They are the most popular Christmas trees in Brazil.

A rock with bite

The Canadian Pacific Railway dumped tons of huge granite boulders at the base of the hill west of Beatteay's Beach to support its rail line, and many of the rocks sank into the mud flats of the beach. One rock that sat atop the others, was bigger than the rest, was shaped like a canine tooth, and it became known as Dog Tooth Rock. At high tide, the water was deep enough to dive from the top of the boulder into the cold Bay of Fundy. Some people also tried to fish from it, but with little success. Dog Tooth Rock was eventually covered over by further dumping that took place when the nearby Digby Ferry Service was established.

An unlikely Civil War spy

Disguised as a man named Franklin Thompson, Sarah E. Edmonds served as a nurse in the American Civil War. She shared her experiences in a book titled *Nurse and Spy*. In 1867 she married west sider Linus H. Seely in Cleveland, Ohio. He grew up in Canada, and worked as a lumber surveyor before immigrating to the United States and marrying Sarah. The couple had three children, but all died. When Sarah passed away in 1898, Linus moved back to West Saint John. In an interview with a local paper in 1906 he said that he was planning to write a second book about Sarah's adventures in the Civil War, but when he died on January 15, 1918, the book had not been completed. He was buried at Cedar Hill Cemetery.